We Just Got On With It

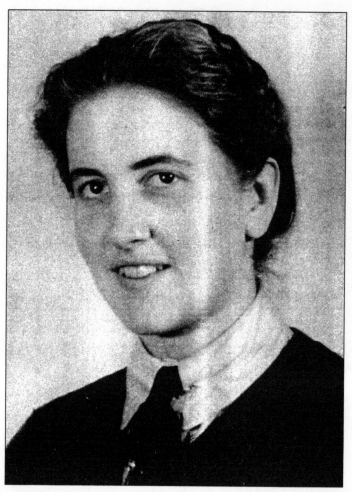

Bette Anderson, member of the Womens Timber Corps 1940–1946

We Just Got On With It

British Women In World War II

by

Bette Anderson

Picton Publishing (Chippenham) Limited

We Just Got On With It
British Women In World War II

© *Bette Anderson*
First published 1994
By Picton Publishing (Chippenham) Limited
Queensbridge Cottages, Patterdown, Chippenham, Wiltshire, England SN15 2NS

Designed and Typeset in Benguiat
By Mike Kelly Photosetting
Avalon, Hartham Lane, Biddestone, Chippenham, Wiltshire SN14 7EA

Printed and Bound by Picton Publishing (Chippenham) Limited

ISBN 0–948251 58 1

Dedication

This book is dedicated with admiration and
gratitude to all those women of wartime Britain . . .
'Who Just got on with it'.

Contents

Contents

Acknowledgements

It would be impossible to list all the people who have contributed towards this book — over the years I must have talked to hundreds of women and read a small library of books. I have folders full of letters and others of cuttings. To all these people who have told me their memories and answered my questions I owe a tremendous debt of gratitude.

The pictures have mostly been supplied by the subjects, who have been most generous in allowing me to use them. I am grateful to the Imperial War Museum, British Rail, NAAFI and Houlton Deutsch Picture Library for permission to reproduce some of their photographs. It is not easy, after 45–50 years, to trace some sources, and if I have infringed any copyrights I offer my apologies.

I should particularly mention the Salisbury Militaria Society, where I was urged to start on the trail which led to this book, at a time when, I think, I was unwilling to regard anything which had occurred in my adult life as a subject for "historical research".

Finally, a word of thanks to Picton Publishing Limited for agreeing to publish this book and for their help throughout its production.

Bette Anderson
APRIL 1993

Introduction

At one of the first exhibitions of Salisbury Militaria Society in which I took part, a small boy, at most 10 years old, was very interested in my Women's Timber Corps uniform; he looked at pictures of the sort of work we did with some puzzlement. 'But isn't that *man's* work?' I agreed that it usually was. 'I thought it was only *now* that ladies wanted to do man's things.' (Women's Lib. was in full flood at the time!) I explained that it wasn't a matter of choice. The men had to go into the Army, Navy and Air Force and somebody had to take over the work they left. He considered this very seriously for some time and finally nodded with a brilliant smile of complete understanding.

'Oh I see – you lot just got on with it – and now they all keep talking about it.'

His observation was more true than he really appreciated – from 1939 onwards it was taken for granted that women would take over more and more jobs which had always been regarded as "man's work".

In fact it was so much taken for granted that unless women actually enrolled in a recognised uniformed service they tend to say they did 'nothing much'. One woman I talked to assured me she was too busy looking after their two small sons and their business to do any war work – on further enquiry I discovered that their business was a coal merchant's and she had literally put on her husband's leather trousers and jacket, taken out the horse and cart and carried on delivering coal, with a pensioner, and a schoolboy on Saturdays and school holidays, to help her. I suggested that she had taken over a man's job, which surely qualified as war work, but she quite seriously replied that in fact she hadn't *really* taken over a man's job as she couldn't manage hundredweight sacks and had to scale down to half-hundredweight loads!

As I have said in the section on Special Operations Executive, there was considerable overlap between SOE, FANY and WAAF. By its nature, SOE was a very secret – and secretive – organisation, and if I have erred in my attributions, I can only apologise and say that I did my best!

My account of the work we did must necessarily be rather superficial, because I want to show how everyone's contribution, however small in itself, contributed towards the war effort. The stories that women have told me for this book are only a very small section but they are typical examples of the way they filled the gaps left when the men were called up. Some of us made jam with the WI, some flew Spitfires and Wellingtons, some sawed pit props for the miners, some drove ambulances in the Blitz, some knitted socks, some fell into the hands of the Gestapo in occupied Europe. Very different service in degree, but if we had not all done what lay within our powers, the outcome of the war could have been different.

To such an extent did we take it for granted that if a job was there to be done, we had to do it somehow, and we did in truth just get on with it!

Run Up To The War

In *British Women Go To War* J. B. Priestley says: 'No country engaged in this war has mobilised its women for the war effort more thoroughly and efficiently than Britain has, and our use of woman power has been one of the unique features of our war record. The need has been very urgent . . . but it must be understood that although the powers of compulsion were there – and had to be there in order that the re-organisation of the people should go through – this wholesale mobilisation of women could not have been successfully carried out unless it was based on a general measure of consent to it; if, in short, most of the women concerned had not been anxious and eager to serve their country and the democratic cause, if there had been anything like a widespread disinclination, a general hostility to this idea of national service, then, powers or no powers, such mobilisation would have been impossible. Co-operation was essential, and from the first it was there. Indeed . . . whenever there has been most grumbling, it has come not from the

reluctance to serve, but from over-eagerness and impatience.'

In fact, so great was this feeling among some women that skills were not being used to the maximum effect in the war effort that in 1941 a book was published raising the issues of under-employment of women in essential war industries – *What Of The Women – A Study Of Women In Wartime*, by Elaine Burton.

Women had proved their value in the First World War and had fought after it to keep their organisations in being, but neither the Army, Navy nor Air Force commands would countenance maintaining women's auxiliary forces in peacetime, and by 1921 the demobilisation of women was complete. The nursing services remained in being and some organisations, independently based, such as FANY, continued their voluntary service and training programmes without a break.

The women who had served during the First World War had no doubt of the value of the contributions women could make in the event of war

56,000 Women were employed by railway companies during the First World War.   *(Wilts Library & Museum Service)*

1

British Red Cross Society in First World War

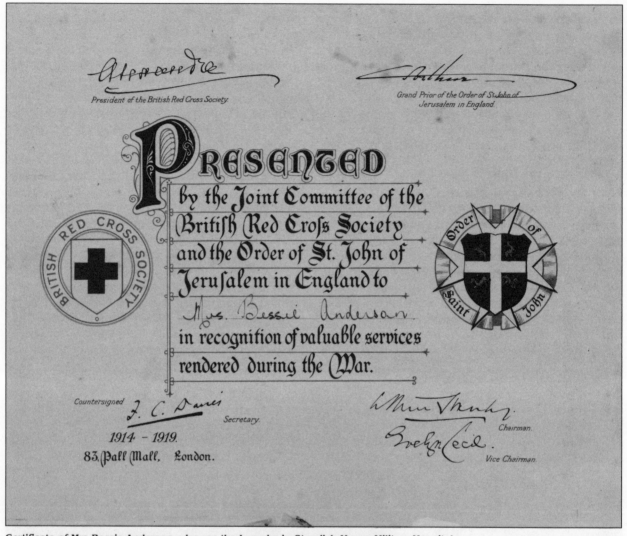

Certificate of Mrs Bessie Anderson, who ran the Laundry in Standish House Military Hospital.

Staff of Standish House Military Hospital, Stonehouse Gloucestershire 1917. Mrs Bessie Anderson is seated on the ground, extreme right.

and, as the likelihood of another war increased in the thirties, they made their own preparations, with or without the encouragement of the Government, and when official policy changed there was already a nucleus of women, trained and organised, ready to build up the services which did such invaluable work during the Second World War. In addition, agricultural camps had given a preliminary introduction to large numbers of women who would later form the basis of the Women's Land Army.

When the Home Office decided that there was a need for a women's organisation to support the ARP, and the Women's Voluntary Service was set up, with Lady Reading as the driving force, the response was immediate and enthusiastic — accurate figures are difficult to find for the first year as most volunteers are referred straight to ARP and were not included in WVS statistics but, apart from these, the enrolments in the WVS by the end of 1938 was well over 32,000.

In the early thirties, Lady Londonderry, who had been a leading figure in World War I, tried to re-activate the Women's Legion, drawing in all the women's organisations which were still in being. She invited Helen Gwynne-Vaughan to become the secretary, at a salary of £500 per year. This was considerably less than she was then earning and she felt that her professional standing was being under-rated, for what she was later to

First World
War Postcard

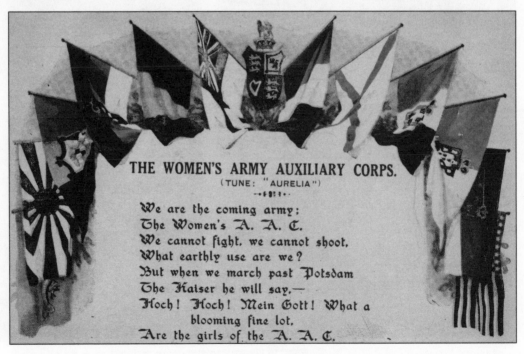

describe as a 'rather grandiose scheme'. However, it was a body which, she felt 'If it is formed, it had better be carefully watched', and with Lady Trenchard's encouragement she did become involved.

Lady Trenchard and her daughter, Belinda Boyle, were also involved, and the first project was an attempt to set up an anti-gas section. This came to nothing when CD was set up and amateur involvement in the field was discouraged.

Helen Gwynne-Vaughan was mainly determined on the setting up of an officer's training wing within the new Women's Legion, not primarily to provide officers for the Legion but to form a pool of trained women to lead any female corps which might later be set up. Through Lady Trenchard, Jane Trefusis Forbes, who had been Women's Volunteer Reserve Transport Officer in the First World War, was drawn into the group and together they

WAAC in France — in and out of uniform!

planned a voluntary organisation which aimed to drill and train in military procedures on the lines of the Auxiliary Women's Corps of 1917–19.

For a while it seemed that unity might be achieved between the independent groups, and at a meeting at the War Office in July 1934 it was agreed:

1. That all women's services should be part of the Women's Legion.
2. That FANY should be the drivers' section.
3. That Helen Gwynne-Vaughan should be responsible for the Officer Training Section.
4. That a new anti-gas section should be formed.
5. That Helen Gwynne-Vaughan should comb the Old Comrades' Associations, the staff of London University and any other organisations for potential candidates.

These proposals awakened considerable interest and, as a result, the Women's Reserve Sub-committee of the Committee of Imperial Defence was set up, but in May 1936 this sub-committee reported that the formation of a reserve of women in peacetime was neither necessary nor desirable. Without official recognition of the overall plan, neither FANY nor VADs saw any value in Lady Londonderry's plan and withdrew.

Meanwhile, Helen Gwynne-Vaughan's cadets had been meeting in Albany Barracks, Regents Park, and were training in 6–8 week courses run on the lines of the 1917–19 women's organisations and she was determined that this activity should be continued, with or without official blessing. In 1938, the first of several camps was held at Abbotshill School, Hemel Hempstead. Lady

Recruiting poster of the period

Maureen Robertson
Women's Land
Army 1917

5

Dalrymple was the head of the school and was also a member of the Women's Legion Council. Mrs Ogilvie Graham and Mrs A. E. Johnson, formerly of the WRAF, acted as Camp Commandants, and Jane Trefusis Forbes was appointed Senior Cadet and was largely responsible for the organisation of the camp.

Now a new name was needed – it was a difficult time; appeasement was the order of the day, and the idea of women training for a possible war was not enthusiastically received. Eventually Jane Trefusis Forbes put forward the title of "Emergency Service" – no mention of war was made in the recruiting; training was to be for "national emergencies".

It was not until Hore-Belisha was appointed Secretary of State for War in December 1937 that the Emergency Service was recognised by the Army

Timber Training Camp, December 1917

First World War – Women's Forestry Corps – Mrs Perret Working Uniform and 'Walking Out' Dress

Council and the Air Council followed suit in 1938. It was then described as a 'voluntary organisation, the purpose of which is to train women as officers for any women's corps which may be employed for any duties other than nursing in a national emergency'.

In 1938 plans were developing to set up women's auxiliaries but the Emergency Service was not given the importance which Helen Gwynne-Vaughan was convinced that it warranted – as its leader, she was not given any preferential treatment over the other women involved.

The scheme was formulated under the title of Women's Auxiliary Defence Service – WADS – and its role was to be 'to relieve personnel of the regular and territorial armies and of the Air Force of various non-combatant duties'. Service was to be for four years, on local or general service; companies would be formed of drivers, clerks and those on general duties. County Commandants would be nominated by Presidents of local Territorial Associations, and in their turn they would nominate other officers. Appointments would be made at War Office, women would be enrolled,

not enlisted. There was no mention of training officers and officers enrolled would not hold commissions. County Commandants would be recorded in a supplement to Army Lists. No mention was made of the Navy in the plans, as the Navy at this stage did not envisage that any women would be needed.

Helen Gwynne-Vaughan soon started making representations to Sir John Brown (among other things, she urged him to change the name – no-one would appreciate being called a WAD – eventually "Auxiliary Territorial Service" was approved).

At the time of the Munich crisis recruits flowed in so rapidly that the TAs could not cope and a monumental muddle developed, and only slowly were the locally formed companies welded into the separate Auxiliary Territorial Service and Women's Auxiliary Air Force, with Helen Gwynne-Vaughan and Jane Trefusis Forbes as their respective heads.

When war eventually broke out, the value of the contribution that women could and should make was no longer in question.

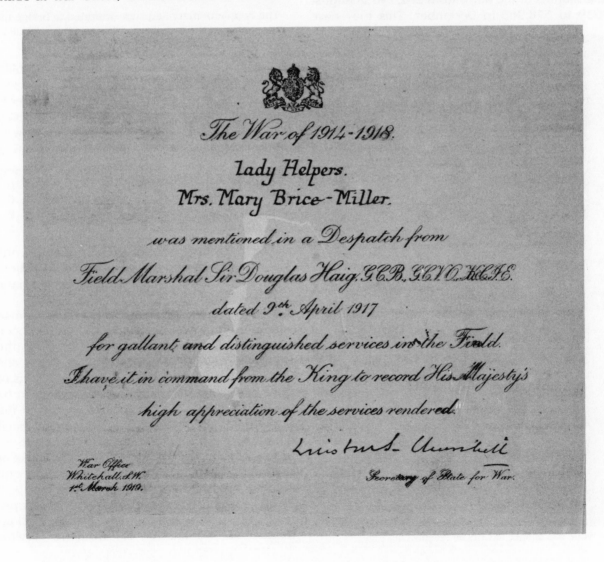

The War of 1914-1918.

Lady Helpers.
Mrs. Mary Brice-Miller.

was mentioned in a Despatch from

Field Marshal Sir Douglas Haig, G.C.B. G.C.V.O. K.C.I.E.

dated 9th April 1917

for gallant and distinguished services in the Field.

I have it in command from the King to record His Majesty's

high appreciation of the services rendered.

Winston S. Churchill

War Office
Whitehall. S.W.
1st March 1919.

Secretary of State for War.

Outbreak of War, Registration and Mobilisation

When war broke out in September 1939 it was accepted that women should be fully involved but even a Ministry of Labour booklet on manpower, published in 1944, says 'Now we come to the most difficult passage in the story: the mobilisation of women for wartime industry.'

In May 1940, agreement was reached with the chief trade unions to admit women to various kinds of work from which they had until then been barred. Women were anxious to play their parts and volunteers came forward in overwhelming numbers. There was considerable frustration as the volunteers, in ever-increasing numbers, were clamouring for work before the necessary plans had been made. In fact, almost incredibly, women's unemployment actually went up in the first months of the war – from 282,148 in August 1939 to 378,983 in December. This may have

Everyone was obliged to carry an Identity Card

been in part accounted for by considerable numbers of women registering as available for work who had previously been living within the family and not included in any statistics, but it must also have indicated a wide reluctance to employ women in work outside the range of what was then generally regarded as "women's work".

Besides employment exchanges, there were three organisations sponsored by the Government:

The Central Register, which existed for the filling of key posts and those of an administrative nature.

The Emergency Register of the Women's Employment Federation – the voluntary contribution made by the federation to the requirements of National Service.

The Supplementary Register, designed to bridge the gap between the ordinary worker and the specialists enrolled on the Central Register.

But, in spite of the women of undoubted ability ready to take up employment, little progress was made at this time; on 7th December, in answer to a question asked by Mrs Irene Ward in the House of Commons, the new intake to various new or rapidly-expanding Government departments was:

	Men	Women
Mines' Department	7	0
Ministry of Shipping	43	0
Ministry of Information	156	8
Air Ministry	149	0

Inspite of its large pool of women of ability, the Central Register was not empowered to submit applications for women for any post for which the department concerned had specified a man.

In 1940, unemployment of women began to decrease, but not before Elaine Burton had been driven to write her book highlighting the problems, *What Of The Women?*, in which she said, 'It is terribly hard to describe the feelings of those of us who were unfortunate enough to be unemployed during the first eight months of the war. I would make the categorical statement that it is impossible for a person safe in a job to understand. No words can bring out the sense of frustration, of sheer impotent anger of someone who has spent the day looking everywhere for a job and has only been confronted with newspaper headlines: "Big Increase In War Effort", "Call-up Accelerated", "Increase of Women's Unemployment".' Can the above be explained? Can there be any reason for such conflicting statements? How can war effort be increased for seven months and the unemployment figures not fall?

And during the year the flow of volunteers for the women's services and the war factories continued to offer more recruits than could be absorbed.

In the first week of the war the *Emergency Powers (Defence) Bill* had passed all its stages and become law, and the same week Regulation 58A under the same Act gave the Minister of Labour and National Service the power to direct each individual in the UK to whatever service might be required of him or her.

At this time the National Joint Advisory Council was set up, composed of representatives of the Trades' Union Congress and the British Employers' Association. Immediately after the passing of the Emergency Powers Bill, Ernest Bevan, Minister of Labour, explained to them the Government's plans for the mobilisation of labour, the Joint Advisory Council pledged their support and the trade unions agreed to relax their pre-war customs so that, for the duration, less-skilled men and women might undertake work which had traditionally been closed to them. At the same time agreement was reached that women, when fully trained to undertake "men's work" should receive the appropriate man's rate of pay.

On the face of it, this left the field wide open for women to undertake whatever work needed to be done, and which lay within their physical powers, but it became progressively more and more clear that, although the latter was less of a restriction than might have been expected, there was still considerable unwillingness to open all doors to them.

Though recruitment continued to fulfil or even exceed demand, by early 1941 it was clear that a more structured mobilisation of the female workforce was needed, and registration was introduced. The Minister of Labour, anticipating more problems than in the call-up of men, appointed a Women's Consultative Committee to advise him, consisting of Mrs Dorothy Elliot, Mrs Walter Elliot, Miss Florence Hancock, Miss Marjorie Maxse, Miss Caroline Haslett, the Countess of Limerick, Lady Megan Lloyd George, MP, Dr Edith Summerskill, MP, Miss Mary Sutherland and Miss Irene Ward, MP. During the period from July 1943 to May 1944, while Miss Irene Ward was abroad, Mrs Cazalet Keir, MP took her place. This committee dealt with any questions arising from registration and call-up of women and concerned itself very particularly with the welfare of women transferred away from their homes.

Ministry of Labour Poster

In spring of 1941 the registration of women began. Any woman who did not have any children under the age of 14 was regarded as available for work. As with men, certain jobs were regarded as "reserved occupations" but there was a further complication – a large number of women were married and had domestic responsibilities and so were further categorised as "immobile" and could not be moved away from their home area. So, to encompass these women, a single woman with no domestic responsibilities, in a reserved occupation, might still be directed to other work in a different district if an "immobile" woman was available to replace her.

To further confuse the issue, another class of woman was also exempt from the requirements to leave her home district – wives of men serving in the forces or the Merchant Navy. Many of these women had no families or homes of their own but, even so, they were classified as "immobile" as it was thought that their husbands would be happier to have it so.

In spite of all these confusing, if not actually conflicting regulations, order grew from the chaotic situation of the early months of the war, as a comparison of 1939 and 1943 statistics is shown overleaf.

Fall in for War Service for Women.

	Women's Aux. Services	Full time C.D.	Munitions	Other Work	Unemp.	Rest of Female Population	Total
1939	–	–	506	4331	302	10901	16040
1943	461	70	1928	4778	36	8747	16020

Figures in 1,000s

Most of the "rest of the female population" were housewives, and a large number of them were doing part-time work, or voluntary service.

'Through these waiting months, a heavy burden is being borne by our people. As I go among them, I marvel at their unshakeable constancy. In many cities their homes lie in ruins, as do many of those buildings which you know and love hardly less than we do ourselves. Women and children have been killed and even the sufferers in hospitals have not been spared. Yet hardship has only steeled our hearts and strengthened our resolution. Wherever I go I see bright eyes and smiling faces, for though our road is stony and hard, it is straight, and we know that we fight in a great cause.

'Here in Britain, our women are working in factory and field turning the lathes and gathering the harvest, for we must have food as well as munitions. Their courage is magnificent, their endurance amazing. I have seen them in many different activities. They are serving in their thousands with the Navy, Army and Air Force, driving heavy lorries, cooking, cyphering, typing, and every one of them working cheerfully and bravely under all conditions. Many are on the land, our precious soil, driving the plough, and making a grand job of it. Others are air raid wardens or ambulance drivers, thousands of undaunted women, who quietly and calmly face the terrors of the night bombings, bringing strength and courage to the people they protect and help.

'I must say a special word for the nurses, those wonderful women whose devotion, whose heroism will never be forgotten. In the black horror of a bombed hospital they never falter, and though often wounded, think always of their patients and never of themselves. And I need not remind you, who set as much store by your home life as we do, how great are the difficulties which our housewives have to face nowadays and how gallantly they are tackling them.'

The Women of England, by HM Queen Elizabeth,
from a broadcast to the women of America, August 1941

Poster encouraging women to work in factories so that men could be released for the armed forces.

11

Housewives

It is more than time for the role of housewives in bringing the war to a successful conclusion to be recognised.

They wore no common uniform, though on a part-time basis they donned many. They were not conscripted, though they could be directed into work to add to their daily chores. It was simply taken for granted that they would provide the back-up (or one might equally well say the backbone) for the whole of the civilian war effort.

J.B. Priestley, in one of his BBC *Postscripts* said, 'It is ten times harder being a decent housewife and mother during a war than it is being a soldier. You have to make a far greater effort to keep going, for you have no training and discipline to armour you. The soldier has his own responsibilities, but when he assumed them he was released from a great many others, whereas his women folk know no such release but have more and more responsibility piled upon them.' He was talking primarily about Londoners during the Blitz, but to some degree his words applied universally.

Indeed, the soldier knew that his food would be supplied – the housewife had to struggle to prepare satisfying meals from ever-decreasing rations and to find time to search and queue for whatever extras were available. Country housewives fared better in some ways but, with husbands away in the forces or working exhaustingly long hours in factories, etc., they probably had to do their own "digging for victory" if they wanted to maintain a supply of fresh vegetables.

Rationing started in January 1940 with 4 oz. bacon, 12 oz. sugar and 4 oz. butter per week – two months later meat followed to the value of 1s. 10d. per week (a little over 9p) and 11d. for children (slightly less than 5p). This later dropped to 1s. 2d. During that summer tea was rationed to 2 oz. per week, margarine 4 oz. and cooking fat to 2 oz. The following year cheese was limited to little more than a mouthful – 1 oz. per week. An old man in the Forest of Dean peered disbelievingly

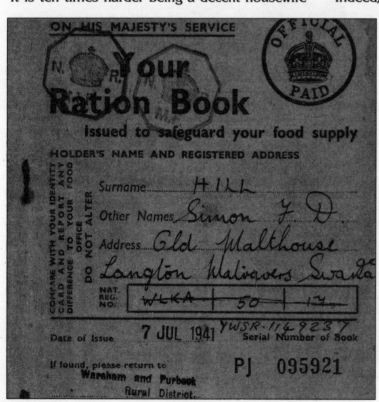

ON HIS MAJESTY'S SERVICE

OFFICIAL PAID

Your Ration Book

Issued to safeguard your food supply

HOLDER'S NAME AND REGISTERED ADDRESS

COMPARE WITH YOUR IDENTITY CARD AND REPORT ANY DIFFERENCE TO YOUR FOOD OFFICE

DO NOT ALTER

Surname ...... HILL

Other Names ...... Simon F. D.

Address ...... Old Malthouse

Langton Matravers Swant...

NAT. REG. NO. ...... WLKA | 50 | 14

Date of Issue ...... 7 JUL 1941   YWSR·114 923 7
Serial Number of Book

PJ 095921

If found, please return to Wareham and Purbeck Rural District...

at his minute allocation and said, 'Be that all I d' get? Then gi' I a biscuit and I'll eat it while you be totting up the bill – 'taint worth dirtying a bit of paper for.'

Later, agricultural workers, miners and heavy industry workers, who might be expected to need sandwiches at work were to have ½lb.

Such was the shortage that at Christmas 1942 Vera Hodgson, a welfare worker in a London East End settlement, recorded in her diary (*Few Eggs And No Oranges*) for Boxing Day, 'Dr H. produced a tin of butter from Johannesburg, and so we all had bread and butter for tea. Magnificent!'

By the beginning of 1942 the points system had arrived – canned meat, fish and vegetables first, followed by rice, canned fruit, biscuits, condensed milk, corn flakes and dried fruit.

As rations became smaller and other items were in ever short supply, there was an endless flow of advice from the Ministry of Food in the press and on the radio in *The Kitchen Front, Food Facts*, etc. But such assurances as a 1941 Ministry of Food advertisement that 'carrot flan reminds you of apricot flan, but has a deliciousness all its own' were not really convincing.

An index is not often humorous but no housewife who had to feed a family will look at the last entry under "Rationing" in Henry Longmates' *How We Lived Then* without a wry smile – 'see also "Shortages".'

But ration cards were always honoured and somehow the housewives managed to keep their children, their husbands, the evacuees, and lastly in many cases, themselves, healthily fed. To their credit, with the help of some special rations of milk, orange juice, etc., children growing up during the war were sturdier and healthier than pre-war.

Another advantage in the forces was the supply of uniforms. The housewife had to cope with clothes rationing. Should she buy a new winter coat and practically nothing else for the year, or make the old coat last another year and replenish stocks of under-clothes, shoes, etc.? "Make do and mend" – darn the socks and stockings until one seemed to be darning the darns.

The
KITCHEN
FRONT

Recipes broadcast during 1942-43 by Frederick Grisewood, Mabel Constanduros and others, specially selected by the Ministry of Food.

SIXPENCE NET   1944 EDITION

Information and recipes featured frequently on radio and in the press.

"Food Facts" appeared regularly in newspapers and magazines

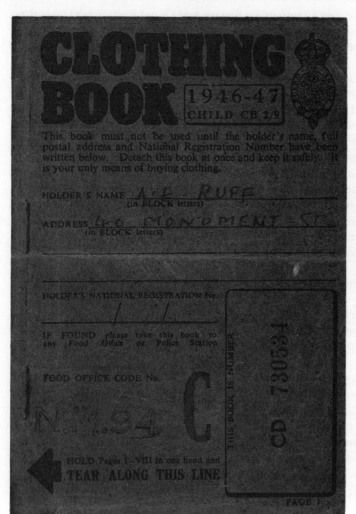

A large item, such as a winter coat used most of a year's allocation of coupons – add a pair of shoes and perhaps material for a summer dress and there was nothing left!

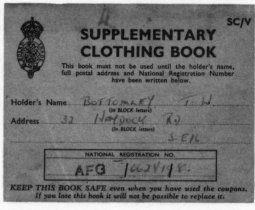

Collage of pattern books. (below)

Wool was distributed from Government centres, and women's groups knitted sweaters, socks, balaclavas, gloves and scarves to supplement factory made uniforms – church groups, street groups, factory staff, WIs, TWGs, senior schools and colleges produced thousands of "comforts" which were returned to the centres and distributed in UK and overseas.

Would the legs of a pair of trousers worn through at the knees or seat make a skirt for a small daughter or shorts for a little son? Unpick the best parts of worn woollies and knit striped sweaters. Look out for coupon-free materials — could a travelling rug be sacrificed to make a coat? Would a saddler sell a length of horse collar lining material? And occasionally — treasure trove indeed — parachute silk or nylon for a blouse.

In London and other bombed cities, they spent their nights in air raid shelters and in the morning came out from their underground refuges to sweep up the broken glass and plaster from fallen ceilings before beginning on the normal daily round, or perhaps to find that their homes had been completely destroyed and that they must start again from scratch with the clothes they wore as their only possessions.

These same housewives will appear again and again in this story in dual roles — they were also the members of the WI, WVS, TWG, ARP, Civil Nursing Reserve, Fire Service, etc. They were munitions workers, car pool and ambulance drivers. They cared for evacuees, ran canteens wherever servicemen were stationed, staffed British restaurants, worked on the railways and the buses, ran nurseries to release other women for war work, organised concert parties to entertain in camps, factories and air raid shelters, knitted thousands of "comforts" for the forces and hospitals. In fact, they turned their hands to any work necessary or desirable to help the "War Effort".

Hilda Doyle with husband Jack pictured at Manthorpe Walk, York in 1940. Hilda had been a nanny pre-1939 but during the war she was a "milk lady" for four years. She did a milk round in York for the Co-op. She started at 6 a.m., walking about six to eight miles a day, with every other Sunday off, for £4 to £6 wages a week. To begin with the two women on the round had to push a barrow, but were promoted first to a horse and float and finally to an electric van. Hilda says, 'When milk was rationed you can imagine the arguments which went on with regards medical certificates and cheap milk, etc.' Milk ladies were not unique to York; they worked in many other places including Plymouth, where Vi Orchard had a pony and float for delivering. The pony was also new to war work. It had previously been a circus pony and when it got bored on the milk round it would break into its old circus routine.

Julie Stevens (pictured above in flowered frock) and Ida Bagg (on the right) worked in the Ordnance Sub-depot in Warminster as civilians. Ida was in the Boots Section and at first could hardly lift a carton of Army boots, but after three months she could 'really sling them around'. Orders had to be got ready for units all around Salisbury Plain. After a couple of years Ida and Julie were transferred to less energetic jobs, working in the barracks' office. Ida dealt with post and Julie worked as an invoice clerk. Ida had moved to Warminster to be near her husband, and Julie met her husband-to-be at the depot.

As more and more men were drafted into the forces, women took over their work in spheres which had traditionally been regarded as essentially "men's work" — postwomen sorted and delivered the mail, women porters handled freight on the railways and in industry, heavy machinery was skilfully handled by women — and at the end of the working day they returned home to their equally important and demanding work as housewives.

It was a never-ending grind — depressing, exhausting and frustrating, but they carried on doggedly. Miss Smith, who was a young teacher in Leicester when the war started, was on duty in a First Aid Post every third night; she was recalled during holidays to run holiday playgroups so that mothers could continue working. Other holidays she worked on a farm. She remembers, 'It was a very full life but often a dreary one, especially when one realised that one would not be young again when it was over. We bottled fruit, salted beans, queued for rations, mended and patched. We slept on stretchers among cockroaches, crickets and black beetles. We learned to use stirrup pumps, we calmed children and put up blackouts. We had occasional treats like going to the cinema or theatre (which were unheated). We achieved very little but we were always *ready* to do much more. And we were *tired*, nearly always. Honestly, the time was filled, but I can't say I did very much for the war effort!'

And Mrs Milburn wrote on 8th April 1944, 'The only thing is to stick it and *stick it* and STICK IT until the war is ended. . .' (Mrs Milburn's diaries).

Major Novello, on a tour of duty in the United Kingdom with the USAF in the 1950s, remembered

A REMINDER

Clothing Coupon Law

1. When shopping over the counter, never cut or tear the clothing coupons out of your book yourself. The shopkeeper must do this.

2. Never offer your shopkeeper loose coupons over the counter. He is not allowed to accept them, and may be prosecuted for doing so.

3. Loose coupons may be sent for goods ordered by post. They must have your name and address on the back – you can cut them out of your book yourself. They must be posted in the normal way. It is illegal to post coupons and order through the letterbox of the shop.

4. It is illegal to sell coupons. People selling or buying them may be prosecuted.

5. Coupons may not be given away to anyone outside your family. If no one in the family needs them, no one else should spend them.

6. Service coupons may not be used by anyone except the person to whom they are issued.

7. A person going into the services may not give his or her clothing book to anyone else. All clothing books must be surrendered to the Military, Naval or Air Force authorities.

8. It is illegal to ask for rationed goods – e.g. silk stockings – from abroad.

9. Coupons must never be divided. If a purchase, e.g. material by the yard, adds up to the fraction of a coupon, you must either make up the coupon with another small purchase such as a handkerchief or two, or lose the value of the coupon.

10. It is illegal to keep the clothing book of a person who has died. It should be returned to the local Registrar of Births and Deaths.

Newspaper report –
29th January 1943

his first visit as a very young sergeant during the war. He said, 'The local priest told our priest about local homes we'd be welcome to visit – I went to two widows in a cute little cottage and very welcome they made me. Mrs Gray's husband was killed in the first war and her son was in a Jap. camp but she was never real sad when we were there. We knew about rationing and tried to be careful what we ate, and help out a bit. Then I wrote my mom to send her a parcel and when she opened it she sat down and cried. I didn't know what I'd done wrong – it looked very ordinary, dull things to me – cans of butter and shortening, sugar and tea and soap, raisins and canned fruit and salmon and ham. I guess I was too young to understand you could cry for pleasure and gratitude as well as for sadness. It was only then I knew how difficult food was – and everything else as well, I guess.'

Good Food Resolutions For 1941

'Food is a munition of war'

Here are some good – food – resolutions for 1941:

I shall try when shopping to remember that food is a munition of war.

I shall know the Food Groups and plan meals which make for health and fitness.

I shall remember that simple foods such as carrots, potatoes and oatmeal satisfy the appetite and are good for health.

I shall not grumble when the butcher does not have the particular joint I want; I shall take the next best thing and be thankful to get it.

I shall use canned foods as little as possible, keeping them as an emergency supply.

I shall use all homegrown fresh fruit and vegetables I can.

I shall waste nothing; even the "left-overs" can be made into appetizing dishes with a little ingenuity.

I shall cheerfully accept the Rationing Orders and never try to evade them in any way.

I shall try to get my local Authority to start community kitchens now.

Newspaper cutting –
January 1941

Christmas 1942

A Toast To The Housewife

At this Christmastide, which symbolises the spirit of family, it would be churlish not to offer a word of praise to the British housewife.

"No extras" is the keynote of our austerity celebration but there is no need to ration our tribute to these unsung womenfolk of Britain.

Without complaint they have borne the burden of wartime shopping with all its difficulties and delays. With limited resources they have prepared tempting meals. Whatever measure of festivity we enjoy this Yuletide will be due to their ungrudging and unselfish efforts.

Many activities

Nor have these devoted women called it a day when their domestic duties have been finished. Thousands have joined fireguard parties. Thousands have thrown open their doors and their hearts to evacuated children. Thousands are mothering essential war workers transferred to vital jobs in distant parts of the country.

Others have inspired to success those mend and make do parties which have been typical of the ways in which improvisation has been necessary. Without their aid the salvage campaign would be a lifeless thing.

Many of these women too, have to carry on, regardless of heartaches engendered by separation from loved ones serving abroad or at a distance from home. But in the midst of their duties seldom is a mail missed or a parcel from home left unpacked.

Heroine of the Hearth

In the near future, thousands will be making an even greater sacrifice of their brief spare time by undertaking part-time work in the factories to speed on the making of the machines of war. By doing so they know that reunion with those away will come the sooner.

Here, then, are true daughters of Britain. The record of Britain's housewives in wartime will go down in history as being the accomplishment of the humdrum with the greatest degree of willingness. There are no medals for these heroines of the hearth; there must be no grudging in our gratitude to them.

Let us, therefore, remember the housewives of Britain, when, this Christmastide, we raise our glasses in tribute to King, country and to all who are helping to make victory ours and to keep us free.

Newspaper cutting –
25th December 1942

Comforts for The Troops

Good work is being done by members of the office staff of the Ford Motor Company to help the boys 'somewhere in France and England'. They have been knitting woollen comforts for the troops, and already four hundred woollen garments have been completed and distributed during the past winter.

This was made possible by a "Comforts for the Troops" fund which was formed by the staff, regular voluntary contributions being made throughout the offices. The fund is administered by a committee of the women staff who themselves help with the knitting.

Apart from contribution to the official distribution centre, special parcels have been sent to the Essex regiment, in which many of the Ford Motor Company's former employees are serving, and I am sure these men must feel happy to know that they are being specially remembered by their firm.

Newspaper item by a female journalist,
April 1940

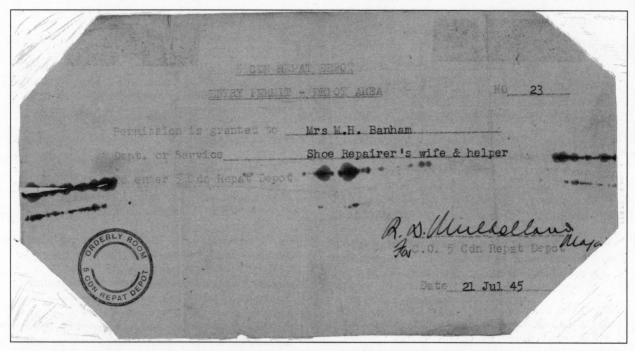

Millie Banham's husband had a contract for boot-repairing in Warburg Barracks at Aldershot. He employed two men. When one of the men was called up Mr Banham asked his wife if she would take the man's place and consequently she worked in his place from 1941 to 1945. She says that it was hard and dirty work and her hands have never been the same since. But in spite of this she remembers it was a happy time, when she felt she was doing something really useful. Each new regiment in the Barracks issued a pass similar to the one reproduced above.

In *Beauty For Ashes*, Winifred Fortescue tells of a girl who had been sent to Cornwall by the War Office to destroy falcons' eggs from nests on the cliffs.

Carrier pigeons had been failing to return to their lofts, and a number of rings had been found in a falcon's nest, indicating that the birds were being destroyed as they approached the coast.

The girl descended the cliffs with only a rope round her, finding footholds where she could, and searching calmly for falcons' nests in the crevices. A Commando officer, who had seen her working on the cliffs near Clovelly, said, 'She goes where some of my young recruits wouldn't dare go. She's got guts, that girl, and no mistake. I take off my hat to her.'

NEWS FROM THE SAVINGS FRONT

The third week of the great Summer Savings Drive brings further encouraging news from every part of the country. Group objectives range from bullets to bombers.

Women, who have been unable to take up other forms of national service, because of their duties in the home are being encouraged to help in the formation of street groups. In some areas Street Group Secretaries are holding conferences to stimulate interest.

The cost of a parachute for each street is the aim of the Savings Group of a South Coast town.

Newspaper cutting –
25th July 1941

When Miss Giltrap was 19 she was in service at Blandford. With her employer she helped to man a canteen on Blandford station. It was not the usual services canteen, which ran on many of the larger stations, but one requested by the War Office and it opened when wanted. Blandford was the last stopping place before Southampton. Word would come through that a troop train was coming and station staff would be told how many men would be on it. The porters put on boilers and a copper, while the helpers turned out, day or night, to serve tea and sometimes sandwiches. They often took letters or postcards for posting in England from the boys. Miss Giltrap remembers vividly the faces of the 18– and 19–year-old boys going away to who knows what fate. After nearly two years of helping with the canteen, Miss Giltrap went into an engineering factory at Southampton, where she worked twelve hours on duty followed by twelve hours off, with two weeks on nights and two on days. She says, 'One night stands out. When going to the air raid shelter at the back of Southampton Water, there was a troop ship going out, and hundreds of voices were singing "We'll Meet Again". The echo is with me still. It was a very clear night, the water was very calm, and there was the drone of planes coming in, and yet those boys could sing.'

Reconciled by Hitler

An Edinburgh woman making a contribution to the National Savings Fund said, 'I have been saving this up to divorce my husband but I think I can stick him better than I can stick Hitler.'

Newspaper cutting –
15th November 1940

Evacuation and Billeting

In addition to the evacuation of schoolchildren from cities, many new factories were built in safe areas, and workers had to be brought in and billeted.

Many Government Departments moved out from London, as did the BBC, and accommodation had to be found for their staffs, as well as for service personnel.

Mrs Arnold, of Lewes, was sent to work in an aircraft factory at Walton-on-Thames. She particularly remembers the kindness of her landlady.

She says, 'I was put in compulsory billets with a very nice couple who had a spare bedroom for taking in lodgers. They really made me welcome. They were so good to me it made my life away from home so much better.' She was really impressed when the couple boiled two eggs for her when she arrived, and gave her a tour of the house even though they were just about to go out.

There were hundreds of landladies all over the country who made a home-from-home for girls directed into work which was often boring and in strange locations far away from family and friends.

Landladies, for the war effort, provided not only lodgings but also contributed much to morale.

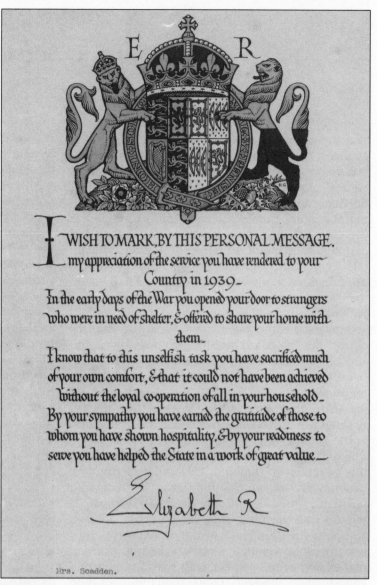

E R

I WISH TO MARK, BY THIS PERSONAL MESSAGE, my appreciation of the service you have rendered to your Country in 1939.

In the early days of the War you opened your door to strangers who were in need of shelter, & offered to share your home with them.

I know that to this unselfish task you have sacrificed much of your own comfort, & that it could not have been achieved without the loyal co-operation of all in your household.

By your sympathy you have earned the gratitude of those to whom you have shown hospitality, & by your readiness to serve you have helped the State in a work of great value.

Elizabeth R

Mrs. Scadden.

Message of thanks, addresses to Mrs. Scadden of Downton, Nr. Salisbury

The evacuees arrive in Downton

Nursing Services

The three armed services had their own nursing services, the only women's services to have had unbroken existence since the 1914—18 war or earlier — Queen Alexandra's Royal Naval Nursing Service, founded in 1884. Queen Alexandra's Imperial Military Nursing Service had its origins in the Crimea when Florence Nightingale took her courageous band of 40 nurses to the base hospitals in Scutari. Princess Mary's Royal Air Force Nursing Service was founded early in 1918, when the first sisters took over the nursing of RAF patients from Army nursing sisters.

Between the wars there was not a large establishment, but as soon as the services prepared actively for war the nursing services made preparations to accompany them wherever they might be sent. The first nursing sisters followed the Army into France within a week of the outbreak of war. Over 1,000 were involved in the evacuation of the British Expeditionary Force in 1940.

A wounded soldier described their service on the beaches of Dunkirk: 'Out on that dreadful beach, with the sun pouring down on them, with German planes continually overhead and shells bursting all the time, they have worked without stopping for days past. If they have slept, they have done so on their feet. Attacked by German planes and even by tanks, with machine-gun bullets whistling all round, I have seen them crawling into the open and dragging wounded men to shelter beneath sand dunes.'

He continued: 'I saw one party of them dressing wounded who were lying out in the open. A plane began bombing. They just lay down by their patients and continued bandaging. They had fetched food and water to assist the men. Angels is the only word you can use to describe them. I have seen some of them killed as they have gone about their work. We have asked them to go back in the rescue ships but they have refused. Each one has said, "We shall go when we have finished this job — there's plenty of time, so don't worry about us." '

Here, and in withdrawals from Singapore and Crete, some of the nurses refused to leave the wounded and were taken into captivity with them.

On the hospital ships, nurses of the Royal Naval Nursing Services carried on with their duties through air and sea attacks. Nine hospital ships were sunk during the war and many more were damaged by enemy action. The nurses, in all cases, put the welfare of their patients before their own safety. Psychologically, the presence of female nursing staff close to battle areas was an incalculable morale booster.

All personnel joining these services had to be State Registered Nurses and either single or childless widows.

Surprisingly, less use was made of Voluntary Aid Detachment personnel than in the 1914—18 war. VADs were largely recruited from British Red Cross Society detachments and St John Ambulance Brigade divisions. They had to have passed examinations in Home Nursing and First Aid, and were regarded as probationer nurses, being employed in any capacity for which they were fitted.

Although they gave devoted service wherever they were sent and provided valuable support in every theatre of war, there was some feeling that

Grace George (above) taught at Chipping Sodbury Grammar School. At weekends and during school holidays she trained as a VAD and worked at Little Sodbury Manor, which was a Military Hospital

H.M. The King meets miss Mary Borden, head of the Hadfield-Spears Ambulance Unit, recently back from France and now with General de Gaulle's Free French Army

Miss Florence Horsbrugh at Mount Gold Hospital, Plymouth, with the Matron, Miss Hutchinson. *(Nursing Mirror)*

Mobile operating theatre
(Nursing Mirror)

Rosemary Chance (right) is in 'Wild Rose' at Princess Theatre, is also VAD at St Luke's, Chelsea; she daily cycles to hospital.
(Photo: Parade)

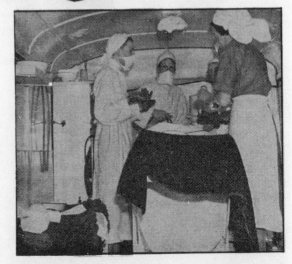

Inside a mobile operating theatre   *(Nursing Mirror)*

To meet the need when hospitals were bombed, or in areas where facilities were inadequate, there were a small number of mobile operating theatres which nurses staffed under difficult and sometimes dangerous conditions.

the detachments were not used to full advantage. They were classified and paid as privates, which lessened the possibility of recruiting specialists such as radiographers, etc.

In 1942 the War Office proposed to absorb the VADs into the ATS but the VADs, and indeed public opinion in general, opposed this measure so vigorously that the proposal was withdrawn. However, the War Office insisted on the abolition of the office of Commandant and the VADs were left without an officer structure of their own. So strong was the feeling against this that about one in five of the VADs resigned.

Meanwhile, with the growth of the Forces Nursing Services, the civilian nursing services were considerably depleted and recruitment to civilian hospitals was a major problem for the Ministry of Health. Before the war a Civil Nursing Reserve register had been instituted. The qualifications for this Reserve were certificates in Home Nursing and First Aid, plus 80 to 100 hours' hospital experience; so it needed considerable dedication to reach the requisite standards on a voluntary basis.

Margaret Freer (who thinks the CNR must be the least written about of women's wartime services) received a letter the day after war was declared, telling her to report to the Public Assistance Institution (the workhouse) at Wellingborough, where some wards were set aside for military use. Pay was not generous – £4 a week, from which £2 was deducted for board and lodgings. Uniform was supplied but laundry had to be paid for. Her duties were divided between the casual wards, for tramps and vagrants, and the military wards. There was a fully-equipped theatre, where Margaret worked for two years out of her five years' service. At the end of the war she was automatically given the grade of SEAN.

Olive Edwards was also sent to a workhouse but in her case its use had been changed and was an Emergency Hospital in Marlborough. They had a number of elderly patients there, evacuated from chronic-sick hospitals in London. There was only one trained nurse on each ward, plus auxiliary nurses.

In 1943 nearly 19,000 Civil Nursing Reserve were serving.

Civilian nursing had its problems – an editorial in the *Nursing Mirror* of August 1940 aired the question of "Midwives in Action": 'The question whether or not a midwife should go out during an air raid is causing a good deal of discussion in various quarters, but not much among midwives themselves. There are reports of medical officers of health issuing explicit instructions to the midwives in their districts to take cover, and the midwives protesting violently.

Civil Nursing Reserve members had both duty and off-duty uniforms. The Nursing Auxiliary initials gave rise to the nickname: 'The Naughty Annies'. Margaret Freer, shared her time between Workhouse *casuals* and Service personnel, who had taken over part of the Wellington Workhouse.

For the duration of the war, the Order of St John of Jerusalem merged with the BRCS. There was no branch of nursing and welfare of war victims in which the British Red Cross Society did not play a part.

WAR ORGANISATION
OF THE
BRITISH RED CROSS SOCIETY
AND
ORDER OF St JOHN OF JERUSALEM

Presented to

Mrs Doreen Elsa Mary Hodges

Junior Lawn Organisation

in recognition of devoted service to
the cause of humanity
during the second world war

1939~1945

George R.I.

Elizabeth R

Sovereign Head,
Order of St. John of Jerusalem.

President,
British Red Cross Society.

Doreen Hodges (2nd from front on the right) worked for the Red Cross packing parcels for prisoners of war, and medical supplies.

Doreen Hodges (centre) in Red Cross prisoner of war supplies store.

Dot Norris was an assistant in a nursery run by the Council at Weston-super-Mare. There were two trained staff with paid assistants, and voluntary helpers did the sewing and cooking. The children were under-fives and were mostly evacuees from London. They also took children while evacuees' mums went into nursing homes to have babies. Dot remembers that the children often arrived dirty, with matted hair, etc. She says, 'I loved bathing them and cutting their hair which I treated with paraffin to get rid of the nits. I dressed the youngsters in nice clothes and they didn't look the same children when I had finished.'

Dot Norris (top left) with the children in the nursery at Weston-super-Mare.

There is, however, very little to argue about on this point, as any midwife knows. If she is wanted urgently by a patient after the sirens have gone, she will use every effort to go. She has, in the country districts during the past winter, gone through ice, snowdrift and flood. She is not likely to be deterred by the fear of falling shrapnel or bombs.' To the midwives, obviously, a completely academic question.

Over 500 hospitals were damaged in air raids and a number of staff were killed. Already over-stretched through shortage of staff and high in-take of casualty patients, as soon as there was an air raid, off-duty nurses had to return to duty to evacuate damaged wards.

The Red Cross also contributed to the nursing care services. They played a large part in the Blood Transfusion Service, maintaining and staffing their own auxiliary hospitals and convalescent homes. With residential nurseries for children they ran nearly 300 establishments. This in addition to the fact that they were giving training in First Aid and Home Nursing and holding the tests which were the qualifications for entry into the Civil Nursing Reserve.

After Civil Defence workers, nurses won more awards for bravery than any other women during the war.

Top right – "Childrens Corner" in a London Air Raid Shelter

Below – The Staff at Sutton Le Hole: Gwendy Knight, Tessa Rowntree, Betty Ashurst, Helen Roake, Alice Hughes, Margaret Watts, Pat Wilson, Betty Fielding. Mona Corrin, Freda Smith, Kathleen Brookhouse, Joy Thornton, Mary England, Marjorie Clark.

As a Quaker, Alma Cureton registered as a conscientious objector and says that she could not join and support the armed forces or work on any war production, but she could undertake work to help relieve some of the suffering caused by war. Her tribunal was satisfied that the work done by the Friends' War Victim Relief Committee was of importance and she worked in a mothers' and children's hostel near Newmarket, and later moved on to working in air raid shelters in London, finishing her wartime service in a hostel for children, many of whom had lost parents in raids on London.

Left – The Students' Hostel at London Hospital, taken over by Friends Quaker Relief

Miss Helen Young, Director of the Presbyterian Hospital, New York City, showing some of the surgical instruments for Britain in answer to the new base hospitals' appeal of 1940. (Above)
(*Nursing Mirror*)

Help from the USA. A new-born baby is dressed in one of the layettes provided by the Red Cross Society for the infants of refugees. (Right)   (*Nursing Mirror*)

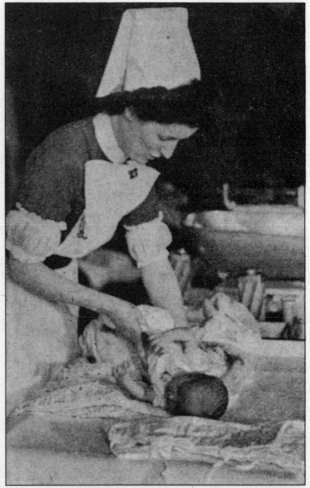

Tin helmets and respirators to hand. Canadian nurses in their common room at No. 15 General Hospital. (above)

Nursing Mirror

(Left) Many women from the Dominions and America came to serve in the United Kingdom. They were equivalent to our ATS, WAAF and WRNS and nursing services. America also supplied and financed an ambulance service consisting of 300 units, ambulances, surgical units and mobile first aid posts. When the USA entered the war the American Red Cross sent units to the UK and a number of British personnel were enrolled. Winifrede W. Phillips (pictured left) joined, first in a voluntary capacity and then as British Staff. She was eventually made a First Lieutenant. She was in charge of the British Staff in clubs and hospitals. Winifrede remembers that 'living with 50 American nurses was quite a problem'.

PoW Camp Starby, Hong Kong. Miss O Franklin, Superintending Sister QARNNS, talking to Admiral Harcourt, Officer Commanding the relieving force 1945.

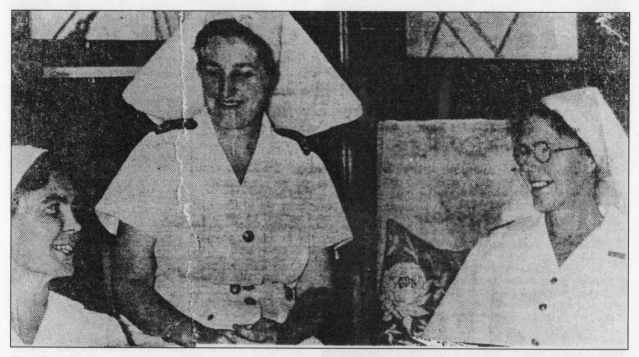

Three Royal Navy nurses who arrived in Sydney in HMS *Oxfordshire*, talk over their internment experiences. They were on the staff of the Royal Naval Hospital, Hong Kong, and after being in other camps eventually reached Camp Stanley. Left to right: Sister G M Griffith, Sister I Rollin and Matron L H Franklin.

HMS *Oxfordshire* admitted over 22,000 patients during World War II.

Patient and QARNNS Nursing Officer pictured in a 'Stately Home of England' used as a
Royal Naval Auxiliary Hospital during World War II.

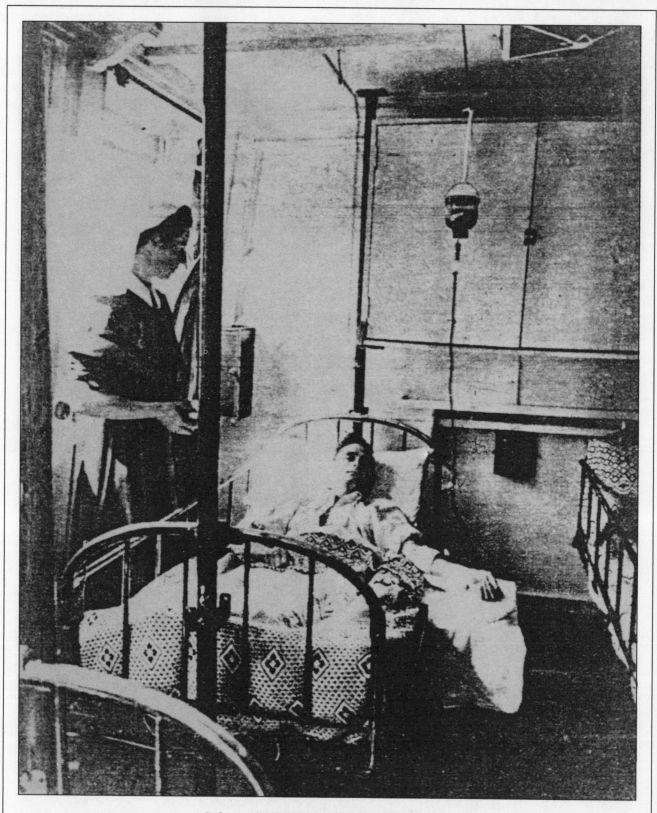

Patient and QARNNS Nursing Officer pictured in a
Hospital Ship during World War II.

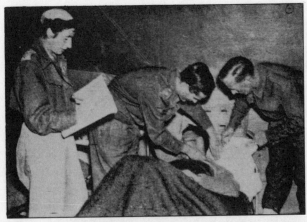

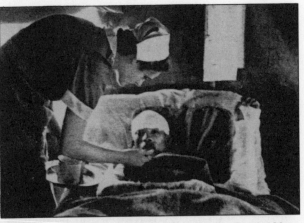

Sister and Medical Officer on daily round in tended ward of a Casualty Clearing Station, Tripoli. (*Photo: Nursing Mirror*)

New Zealander, Sister Murray giving medicine to South African native soldier between Cario and Tripoli. (*Photo: Nursing Mirror*)

Left – Del Monica Hotel, Cape Town – en route for Middle East.
Sister Brennan 2nd from left, Sister Gilligan 4th from right, Sister Crawforth 2nd from right, QAIMNS.
(*Photo: Weismann, Cape Town*)

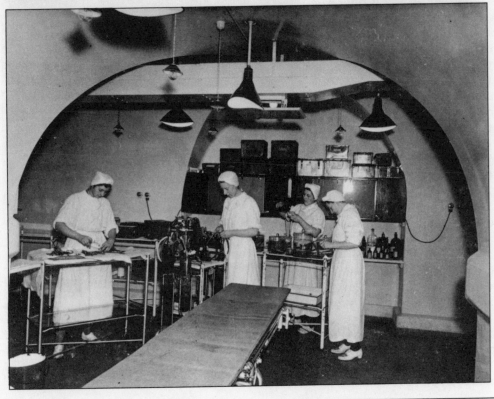

Left – Basement operating theatre, RN Hospital Haslai World War II.

Civil Defence and Air Raid Precautions

The first move towards organising air raid precautions came early in 1937, with an appeal for 800,000 volunteers to act as air raid wardens in case of air attack – the Home Office directive saw 'no intrinsic reason why women should not perform the duties'. There was not an enthusiastic response to this first appeal, however, a year later, when the threat of war was more real, a renewed appeal had better results.

In March 1938 the WVS was launched to direct women into the most appropriate services, and Lady Reading called on 'every kind of woman in every kind of sphere of life – to prepare patiently and thoroughly – a protection – for our loved ones and our homes'.

In July 1939 the Civil Defence Act was passed, and by then Sir John Anderson was able to say that it was 'putting the yoke on a willing horse'. Volunteers came in steadily and were trained, but it was soon realised that a voluntary service would not suffice for the devastating air attacks which were anticipated as soon as war started, and payment of £3 per week for men and £2 for women in wartime was authorised and they were mobilised full time on 1st September. Attitudes were still ambivalent – ARP personnel trained hard and prepared for what was to come but during the "phoney war" it was regarded as a soft option – wardens, ambulance drivers, AFS personnel, etc. were regarded by some as parasites drawing their wages and doing nothing to earn them.

From the outset, women played a considerable part in this field at Government level – Civil Defence in general was under the control of the Ministry of Home Security and Ellen Wilkinson was Parliamentary Secretary of this department from October 1940 to the end of the war. Some aspects such as the casualty service, health in shelters, etc. were vested in the Ministry of Health, where Florence Horsbrugh was Parliamentary Secretary throughout the war. All over the country women were sitting on the vast majority of invasion committees.

Women were accepted as wardens, ambulance drivers, clerks and storekeepers and to staff first aid posts and rest centres – the interval between the declaration of war and the first air raids gave the Civil Defence services valuable time to streamline their organisation and, by the time the air raids on London began in June 1940, over 50,000 women were employed full time and many more on a part-time basis. By 1942 the manpower

shortage had reached crisis point and full-time workers were decreased sharply, to be replaced by greatly increased numbers of part-timers – at the peak there were 80,000 women employed full time, but by 1944 the figure had dropped to 56,000 backed up by 350,000 part time.

Joyce Dickson was an air raid warden at Post 002, Eltham, London, when she was in her late teens. Eltham was one of the areas which merited the award of the Defence Medal. She remembers being on duty alone at night outside a surface shelter occupied by families. She was scared of the dark and the possibility of mice and such wildlife which might be at large. She sat on the top rail of a gate, much happier when she had the company of searchlights, 'the occasional bomb, and other noises off'. One very unpleasant incident Joyce remembers was hurrying to the post when a landmine was dropped. She ran into an injured lady with an eye hanging on her cheek. Joyce was very proud that she did not faint.

Florence Morrison was an air raid shelter inspector in Edinburgh. She wore a navy uniform, and was supplied with a torch. She found the job at times hilarious and sometimes quite frightening. There was quite a labyrinth under North Bridge and the streets round about, and the traffic overhead could be noisy. Florence never knew what she would find – sometimes drunks and often courting couples (particularly after the American troops arrived, she recalls). It was quite a well paid job, fortunately, as Florence's husband died in 1942, leaving her with two daughters to bring up.

As laid down in a Home Office memorandum of 1937, the duties of wardens were legion; they were: 'to know the organisation of air raid services in their locality and the means by which they should communicate with them, to advise persons in the street after an air raid warning where to find the nearest shelter, to report immediately the fall of bombs; to report fires to the fire brigade; to report at once if the presence of gas is suspected and if provided with local gas alarm, to sound it; to reconnoitre the extent of bomb damage caused and supplement their report as soon as possible by further details; to assist occupants of damaged buildings to find new shelter; to guide the police, fire brigade, first aid parties, rescue parties, etc. on arrival to the scene of damage, and convey messages and render any other assistance that may be required by police or fire brigade officers, to assist in every possible way to prevent panic and set an example of coolness and steadiness among their neighbours; to help householders or the personnel of fire posts to fight incipient fires pending the arrival of the fire brigade.'

At the height of the Blitz one warden in six was female and they certainly carried out their duties with remarkable 'coolness and steadiness'. Civil Defence became a part of everyone's daily life in one way or another in the towns and cities which were bombed, and the proportion of the burden which fell on the women increased steadily.

By December 1940 it was clear that fire bombs were a major factor in the destruction of property and fire guard-duty was made compulsory for men. When the Minister of Home Security, Hubert Morrison, was asked if it was anticipated that women would be included, he issued the following statement: 'I have been asked whether women are to undertake fire bomb fighting. This is dangerous work – for that matter so is work with the ambulance service. Time has gone by when women could be kept away from dangerous work in defence of this country, and if they are ready for service, I am not going to say "no". The women of this country have shown that when air raids come they have just as high courage and just as steady nerves as men. It may be that the idea of defending their homes or the businesses where they work as frontline fighters will make a special appeal to them.'

It was not made compulsory until 1942, but in the interim women volunteered and took part in fire watching duties in large numbers. In fact, fire bombs which were dropped in huge quantities were regularly dealt with by householders as and when necessary – the oldest woman to extinguish one was 90, and at the other end of the age scale, school children played their part in putting out fires – when emergencies arose, everybody who was able played her part, with no reference to sex or age.

At this time some 470,000 people were sleeping in shelters each night. Shelters and the underground were soon well organised – shelter wardens, who were responsible for the order and welfare of these huge subterranean communities, included a fixed proportion of women. These women were often drawn from among the shelterers – emerging by sheer force of personality from those around them. In addition to the immediate welfare of the shelters they undertook responsibility for cleaning and disinfecting the shelters, checking emergency lighting and ventilation, ensuring supplies of drinking water and checking that entrances were clear. They also instigated entertainments, both for children and adults – community singing, talks, handicraft classes – the range was wide enough to suit all tastes.

To deal with casualties, many women served as ambulance drivers and staffed first aid posts. To help those who had lost their homes, rest centres offered temporary accommodation, clothing and food, and provided the necessary advice and instructions for coping with the various departments issuing replacements for lost coupons,

Dorothy Cosgrove joined the Civil Defence in Winchester and worked in Hants Control. This centre was open 24 hours a day, taking reports from the Observer Corps, plotting the position of planes coming in and passing the information on to the services. At first, Dorothy worked on the night shift, alternating between 5 p.m. to 1 a.m. and 1 a.m. to 9 a.m. With the complete blackout, and in a barrack town, the walk from the centre was not pleasant, and after one or two scares she managed to change to the day shift.

arranging for temporary repairs to houses, etc. Whatever need arose through enemy action, help was quickly forthcoming and in every case women showed their initiative, their organisational abilities, their courage and their dogged persistence against seemingly overwhelming odds.

Kathleen Finlayson (who had been in the Women's Forestry Corps during the 1914–18 war) drove a mobile bath and laundry unit in London during the Blitz. She remembers, 'A six and a half ton lorry carried a ton of water, an oil-burning engine and Clarkson boiler which heated the water. The bath unit had three compartments – dressing rooms for five people each end, and five shower-baths in the centre. While five people were showering, having undressed at one end, five more were undressing at the other end, ready to go in as soon as the showers were vacated, and so on from alternate ends. These units were first used for firemen, police and rescue units – they did not function during a raid, but were ready for action as soon as the all-clear sounded. It was a rule that the water should always be mains drinking water, so that it could also be used for hot drinks. The duties of the bath units (a team of three women and a man) soon widened and they set up near schools and the children bathed under the supervision of teachers and WVS – sometimes as many as 300 children a day.'

A Year of Housewives Service
Warminster's Splendid Contribution

It is just over a year since the Housewives Service was started in Warminster and some useful work has been done in this quiet sector of the home front. The framework of the service is simple: Chief Housewife at the head, a Sector Leader for each ARP post and Key Housewives, each in charge of a group of twelve to twenty houses. Every house in the town has been visited and each Key Housewife has taken a miniature census of her group, with lists of occupants of each home (special note being made of small children or infirm or aged people who would need extra help in case of a raid). A record has been made of the defence duty each housewife is prepared to do in case of emergency, in itself a cure for panic or the blues. One may have promised to care for the blind neighbour, another will help with the nearest baby's gas mask or will open her cottage as a shelter for the homeless. The Key Housewife knows what expert first aid help she can depend on, who has a supply of bandages and gas ointment and who is running the cleansing stations and where they are. Any information wanted by the Wardens is gathered by the Key Housewife and added to the records of the Post.

Two sectors have built emergency cooking stoves and others are following suit. Cleansing stations have been organised according to Wardens' requirements and stirrup pump teams have been trained. Although the talks arranged by the ARP bodies in gas, civil defence and bombs have been rather sparsely attended, group talks on first aid, with VAD instructors, have been popular. The women must meet in one another's houses to practice bandaging and so on, sometimes persuading their Wardens to act as casualties. Each sector has its own methods, adapted to the local housewives' scanty free time, and the most successful are those where the Wardens accept co-operation and give encouragement. In one sector, at least, the Sector Leader and her Key Housewives are invited to attend a monthly Wardens' meeting, a privilege of which they are proud. Now and then, not often, for all have a full time job in their own homes, the Sector Leaders meet to compare notes and discuss difficulties.

Busy as all the townswomen are – Boreham villagers too – there are few who do not take to heart the necessity of playing their small part in Civil Defence. Even in those regrettable cases where Wardens do not smile on Housewives, the unobtrusive preparations go on for the day that everyone hopes will never come to Warminster and will go on, in odds and ends of time snatched from cooking and washing up and getting the children off to school, till the Cease fire! sounds.

Written anonymously – July 1943

The laundry units had two washing machines, wringer drying cabinet, ironing boards, two sinks and water heaters. They hitched up to the mains water supply and, where possible, the electricity supply, though they had their own generator when necessary. Anyone who lacked facilities at home – and water, electricity and gas supplies were frequently lost – could take in 15 articles for washing – if they could take them home to finish off, that was that, but if not the WVS co-operated with ironing.

Kathleen Finlayson particularly remembers the air raid victims who came to have baths. While their clothes were hastily washed, ironed and mended by the WVS, or perhaps replaced, they sat wrapped in blankets until they could be re-clothed.

They always had a cheery welcome at the docks where the firemen would tell them to have a rest – 'a real good cuppa, well-buttered penny buns, in comfortable chairs, with plenty of daily papers and women's magazines,' while the men ran the unit, had their baths, scrubbed out and packed up again – 'they were a grand lot of men.'

And finally when they set up outside baby centres, 'One day we washed over 1,000 nappies and cot sheets. It was a day of days to see garden after garden with lines full of nappies – I think it was the collected washing of three or four babies' homes, plus a breakdown at the usual laundry.'

Compared to the conditions in London and other bombed cities, civil defence duties in country districts were negligible – a careful check on the efficiency of the blackout and the readiness of all services in case of need. Training in gas precautions, fire fighting, etc. was carried out, and a force of personnel was ready to deal with any emergency which might arise – the network over the whole country was planned and maintained in readiness throughout the war. I took an anti-gas course in the Forest of Dean and qualified to "assist an instructor" – I played patience through night time fire watching sessions in the Wiltshire countryside and took fire-fighting lessons in a Devon village. Everywhere there were volunteers prepared to ensure that any "incident" would be swiftly and efficiently dealt with.

Messenger Identity Card.

Bette Anderson took an Anti-Gas Training Course and qualified as an assistant instructor.

Auxiliary Ambulance Service

Ambulance driving became very much a woman's preserve — when the Auxiliary Ambulance Service was set up in 1938 it was in fact the Women's Voluntary Ambulance Service and took only women volunteers. It was set up and organised exclusively by women until shortly before the war broke out, and in the first year most of the training was carried out by women.

At first, recruits were mainly middle-and upper-class women, most of whom had never worked for their living, or who had given up work on getting married. In the '30s cars were much more of a luxury than today and the proportion of women who could drive was comparatively low (in 1939 there were fewer than two million private cars licensed).

Initially, volunteers were enrolled only as drivers and the ambulances were mainly make-shift vehicles — either converted commercial vans, or cars with trailers fitted with racks to take stretchers. These were very gradually replaced by purpose-built ambulances.

The training was thorough — it was essential for every driver to know her district in detail. In towns and cities this entailed familiarity with every road so that alternative routes could be taken rapidly in case of bomb damage. They had to know every ARP centre and warden's post, first aid post, ambulance station and hospital, gas decontamination centre and rest centre.

In country areas where it might be necessary to cover wider areas to go to crashed planes, or to give assistance if nearby towns were bombed, it was essential for drivers to be able to map read with confidence and to drive at night with minimal lights (headlights during the war were less than

Photograph taken of the Barrow Castle Ambulance Depot, Bath. Mrs Head (left) learned to drive on a converted van, which she described as 'a real old bone-rattler', and was fitted with racks for stretchers. She was a Civil Servant, working full time and was on duty at the ambulance station one night a week. In addition, she took Red Cross first aid lessons. Before she was allowed to drive she had to pass a strict test and says that Mr Tuddenham was a very tough examiner.

today's weakest side lights) and no signposts.

During 1938 and '39 the Auxiliary Ambulance Service joined in all ARP exercises and, during the summer of 1939, men were also accepted as volunteers but throughout the war there were almost twice as many women drivers as men.

The early volunteers were only drivers but, later, women served as attendants. Drivers were responsible for checking and cleaning their vehicles, while attendants dealt with the equipment. While training was thorough, there was at first still a tendency to regard women as the "weaker sex" – in one London borough, where exercises were accompanied by records of exploding bombs, the volume was turned down when ladies were involved. When the bombing started, the ambulance crews proved that such refinements were totally superfluous – in fact, among the earlier George Crosses awarded to women were two to an ambulance crew, Mrs Clark and Mrs Hepburn, who showed outstanding courage and coolness in rescuing a badly injured man in an area where further explosions were likely to occur.

Barbara Charman learned to drive before the war – a much more unusual accomplishment then than it is now! She wanted to go into the ATS but was told that no drivers were required. She was so determined to use her driving skill that she decided she would only go into an organisation which needed drivers, and so she became an ambulance driver in ARP.

This picture is of her group on 3rd September 1939, in rather sketchy uniforms – 'What a motley crew we were,' says Barbara. She later became a Section Leader and was driving heavy ambulances. The vehicle in the top picture is an Army type ambulance which was donated by the people of Barbados. Barbara was in Portsmouth throughout the war, where the work of ambulance crews was no sinecure. She has memories of many frightening spells of duty during air raids, but feels that she was able to do a worthwhile job.

Fire Services

In the Auxiliary Fire Service, as in many other spheres, the enrolment of women was at first regarded as quite unjustifiable – too hard, too dangerous – in short "man's work". In fact, the AFS was not welcomed at all by the regular fire service units, who felt that their jobs might be threatened.

The AFS was formed early in 1938, and women were recruited as drivers, clerks, telephonists and watch-room staff – 40 hours' training was given to the watch-room personnel. Recruits came in quickly and, by the outbreak of war, 5,000 women had enrolled in the London AFS alone, and a great deal of the control room duties was being carried out by women. As calls on the service increased during air raids, women took over an ever-widening range of duties, though they were not, in the main, used for direct fire fighting. Incendiary bombs were comparatively easy to extinguish but if left to take hold could cause devastating fire damage, and here women gave sterling service.

In 1941, the autonomous local fire brigades and the Auxiliary Fire Service units were combined into the National Fire Service and, as manpower became more and more of a problem, women became motorcycle despatch riders and drove lorries and store vans, etc. They took over stores and became mechanics and hose repairers. A large number became Mobilising Officers, taking responsibility for assessing messages about fires and ordering out the appropriate units and equipment.

Women AFS/NFS personnel won a large number of awards for bravery; in the first couple of years, during the heaviest of the bombing, a George Medal, 17 BEMs and nearly 40 commendations for bravery. A typical example was that of two young telephonists at a London fire station who, during a raid, stayed at their phones while the building itself was on fire. They did not leave until the lines went dead, when they ran to the nearest public

National Fire Service officers at Divisional HQ, Kingsworthy Court, Winchester.

phone box and re-established contact with their control centre, then for three hours, throughout the raid, one acted as telephonist while the other took messages between the phone box and the station fire officer. They were both awarded the BEM.

In Portsmouth also, telephonists were awarded BEMs for their coolness and courage in staying at their posts during heavy raids.

The photograph (above) shows a group on the steps of Turret House at Felpham, near Bognor Regis, Sussex and includes Carole Manley, Meg Grimmett, Joan Murchall and F. Huffam.

Firewoman 872772 Joan Muchall (left) served for four years in Lancashire before moving south in readiness for D-Day. Still in her early twenties, she was on duty in sole charge of Horsham Fire Station at night. She says 'If there was a fire, I put the bells on and called the butcher, the baker and the candlestick maker who manned the machines. They came running from all directions to answer the call. I never felt in any danger (except from the enemy) when manning the watch room at night alone.'

Firewoman Joan Muchall.

Betty Gifford joined the Fire Service and was sent to Kingsworthy Court, near Winchester (Divisional Headquarters). After a course in London she was made a leading firewoman. The control rooms were staffed 24 hours a day and the switchboard staff alternated between one week on days and one week on nights. After a while Winchester DHQ had a wireless car, and Betty was on a wireless training course. She put up a second stripe and trained other girls for the work as well as attending all fires in the district. Although she never got used to working odd hours, she enjoyed the work. She says they had an interesting social life and suffered very little bombing even though there were Army and RAF targets nearby. Betty is pictured above with colleagues at Kingsworthy Court.

Fire-fighters – husband and wife – the Herberts.

NATIONAL FIRE SERVICE
CERTIFICATE OF SERVICE

Name (in full) .... Joan Cossey Oliphant Herbert ....

National Fire Service No. 845046 .... Date of discharge .... 30th August, 1945.

Rank on discharge .... Firewoman ....

Cause of discharge .... At own request ....

	WITH LOCAL AUTHORITY FIRE BRIGADE		WITH NATIONAL FIRE SERVICE	
WHOLE-TIME SERVICE	from	1.9.39	from	18.8.41
	to	17.8.41	to	30.8.45
PART-TIME SERVICE	from	12.12.38	from	
	to	31.8.39	to	

31st August .... 19 45.

By direction of the Secretary of State

41

Home Guard

One might almost say that the powers-that-were had a love-hate relationship with women in the Home Guard.

At the beginning of the war, in many areas women undertook daytime patrol duties for the Home Guard (or Local Defence Volunteers, as they then were). It was difficult for men to cover all the daylight hours when many of them were working very long periods on essential work. With the expectation of parachutists or invasion, LDV patrols were regarded as an essential service, so women took over. On Dartmoor, a mounted patrol had been organised and women undertook this patrol in pairs from dawn to dusk, notifying police or Local Defence Volunteers if they saw anything suspicious or irregular.

In October 1941 the War Office stated firmly that women were not eligible for enrolment in the Home Guard in any capacity but, at the same time, suggested that they should not be discouraged from helping unofficially in non-combatant duties.

When their activities with the Home Guard were curtailed, in some areas a parallel organisation, never officially recognised, began to appear. This was "The Women's Home Defence Corps". In this the volunteers learned to shoot and undertook training in signalling, reconnaissance and other activities which would be of value should the defence of their locality become necessary.

Ruth Colyer joined the Women's Home Defence Corps in Cambridge, where she learned to handle

Margaret Barnett (née Allen) and a friend joined the Home Guard in Edgware, Middlesex, soon after they left school in 1943. They were 17, and Margaret says she thinks they joined more out of a sense of adventure than an overwhelming patriotism. She remembers being rather bored drilling on the parade ground and learning morse code, but enjoying rifle practice and sending and receiving telephone messages. The photograph was taken when the Women's HG Auxiliary formed a guard of honour outside the church at the funeral of one of their members who had been killed in a road accident. (Margaret is wearing the light skirt.) The Women's Auxiliary were issued with forage caps, ties and shoulder titles but no uniform, and Margaret says that they were indignant at not being issued with tin hats, as they had a mile to walk to and from the depot and there was sometimes shrapnel falling around them.

a rifle. She continued until pregnancy intervened. 'Rifle shooting necessitated lying prone on the ground, and when pregnancy caused my stomach to be enlarged I became a bit rocky when lying on it, so I had to abandon firing a rifle,' she says. She then had to withdraw from the Corps (she later joined an amateur dramatic group touring camps in the locality).

About 20,000 women enrolled in the Corps, and there were between 200 and 250 units formed, ready for action should they be needed.

In April 1943, the War Office again changed course, withdrew its ban on women and allowed their enrolment in strictly non-combatant capacities. They were not to be issued with uniforms and would not come under military law. They would, however, be allowed to wear brooch badges with the letters HG surrounded by a wreath. At this stage they became "nominated women" – a strangely non-committal description which, a year later, was replaced by "Home Guard Auxiliaries".

This ambivalence was summed up in a letter to the press, saying, 'They might de-grease rifles but not fire them; they might look after uniforms but not wear them; they might cook rations but in no circumstances eat them.'

Officially or unofficially, a large number of women carried out clerical duties, acted as telephonists, storekeepers, drivers, etc. and when their enrolment was, however grudgingly, permitted their (official) numbers increased rapidly. At the peak in 1944 they stood at over 30,000.

There is no way of knowing how many women played their part in supporting the Home Guard but it is indisputable that in spite of discouragement from the "top brass" there was a very considerable female back-up. If it was necessary to protect their homes, women were not prepared to stand by and do nothing, whatever the War Office might have said.

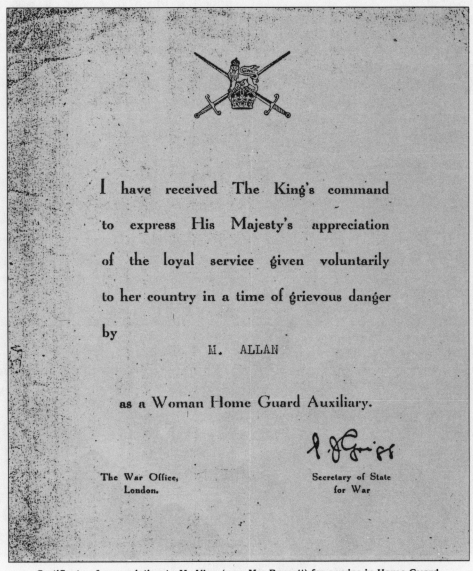

I have received The King's command to express His Majesty's appreciation of the loyal service given voluntarily to her country in a time of grievous danger by

M. ALLAN

as a Woman Home Guard Auxiliary.

The War Office,
London.

Secretary of State
for War

Certificate of appreciation to M. Allan (now Mrs Barnett) for service in Home Guard.

Women's Voluntary Service

What did the Women's Voluntary Service *not* do during the war years?

In 1938 it was decided that a comprehensive organisation of women was needed to recruit women and direct them into the most appropriate branches of ARP. It would need to work closely in association with the Home Office and local authorities, be strictly non-political and non-sectarian. For various reasons none of the existing organisations filled the bill, so Lady Reading was asked if she would start "something special". It was not long before the slogan "the ladies who never say no" was coined but, such was the respect the WVS earned, this dubious slogan never resulted in the ribald connotations that might have been expected.

So, on 18th June (the anniversary of the Battle of Waterloo) the WVS was officially launched. The country was divided into 12 regions for civil defence purposes and the WVS organisation followed the same pattern. Their local branches were always set up with the approval, and under the instruction of, local councils. In May 1940 Lady Reading addressed an Order of the Day to all the County Organisers, 'Please do not hesitate to take such lead as is demanded of you . . . WVS is looked upon as a strong, efficient machine which can carry an immense load.'

The uniform of the WVS was designed by Digby Morton, a leading London couturier. As other women's organisations wore black, navy, blue, khaki and grey, the WVS wore green. Because some people regarded green as an unlucky colour it was blended with grey. The dark red blouse added a touch of colour. It was all severely practical. The greatcoats could be slept in and still looked neat because they did not show the dust. The straight skirts needed no ironing. The blouses

WVS group, Stanmore, Middlesex,
Standing: Wright, Weary, Griffiths, Cox, Wyley. *Seated*: Crowhurst, Wilkie, Ryalls. *(Photo: Dixon Studios)*

44

SEPTEMBER

Sun.	Mon.	Tues.	Wed.	Thur.	Fri.	Sat.
·	·	·	·	·	·	1
2	3	4	5	6	7	8
9	10	11	12	13	14	15
16	17	18	19	20	21	22
23	24	25	26	27	28	29
30	·	·	·	·	·	·

The main responsibility for organising the evacuation of children rested with the WVS — refreshments had to be provided en route, as journeys were often long and slow.
(WVS calendar)

"UNDER FIVES" EVACUATION

JANUARY

Sun.	Mon.	Tues.	Wed.	Thur.	Fri.	Sat.
·	1	2	3	4	5	6
7	8	9	10	11	12	13
14	15	16	17	18	19	20
21	22	23	24	25	26	27
28	29	30	31	·	·	·

The "Under Fives" were a special responsibility, and a recurring one! When air raids were reduced in intensity many children returned home, only to be evacuated again when raids were recommenced.
(WVS calendar)

had neither collar nor tie, which made for speed in dressing, and the short sleeves did not need to be rolled up. The very plain "schoolgirl felt" hats could be, and were, worn at any angle or shape. They were justified by Lady Reading as allowing the women to express their individuality.

At first, the task of WVS was recruiting women for ARP and they were passed straight on to the appropriate arm without being enrolled in the WVS. It is, therefore, impossible to estimate the true number of volunteers, but 32,000 had enrolled in the WVS by the end of the year.

The first major assignment was planning for the evacuation of women and children from the major cities and coastal areas. Evacuation officers were appointed in every area likely to be used for reception purposes. Committees were formed to deal with this mass movement of people who would be unable to plan or organise for themselves, so that when evacuation had to be put into operation it was accomplished with creditable smoothness. There were, of course, many unforeseen problems but, with endless patience, ingenuity and long hours of hard work, most of them were satisfactorily solved.

When a new need arose which did not fall clearly into any departmental responsibility, it seemed that the WVS immediately sprang to mind. Bauxite, coming mainly from Jugoslavia, was badly needed for aircraft. It was the chief commercial source of aluminium. Lord Beaverbrook rang the Chairman and asked if the WVS would organise the collection of aluminium pots, pans and other items. Lady Reading made a broadcast appeal and within hours the contributions were pouring in. The piles of salvage grew almost faster than they could be hauled away, and the final total was over 1,000 tons.

When enemy aliens were interned, the WVS were involved with the arrest of females. They staffed collection centres and acted as escorts on trains.

After Dunkirk, with the minimum of foreknowledge of what would be needed, the WVS met the returning troops, provided canteens, rest centres and along the railway routes provided teas, sandwiches, etc. for the trainloads of troops passing through. They collected and distributed shirts, socks, plus other clothing to replace lost kit. They also washed and mended at incredible speed. Many of them didn't go to bed for two or three nights, snatching a few hours' sleep as and when they could.

After the evacuation of the troops from Dunkirk there was a flood of refugees from the Continent, and for these a reception service was needed. The WVS provided interpreters. Local clothing depots were set up. The Refugee Clothing Centre in Eaton Square alone dealt with 11,000 items of clothing before it closed.

DECEMBER						
Sun.	Mon.	Tues.	Wed.	Thur.	Fri.	Sat.
.	.	.	.	.	.	1
2	3	4	5	6	7	8
9	10	11	12	13	14	15
16	17	18	19	20	21	22
23	24	25	26	27	28	29
30	31	.	.	.	.	.

The majority of main-line railway stations had services' canteens — on the larger stations open 24 hours a day. WVS undertook the organisation of most of them.

(WVS calendar)

EVACUATION BASE KITCHEN

AUGUST						
Sun.	Mon.	Tues.	Wed.	Thur.	Fri.	Sat.
•	•	•	1	2	3	4
5	6	7	8	9	10	11
12	13	14	15	16	17	18
19	20	21	22	23	24	25
26	27	28	29	30	31	•

Mobile kitchens were set up wherever large numbers of evacuees were moving — entailing handling heavy boilers and 60 lb. containers.
(WVS calendar)

RECEPTION OF EVACUEES

OCTOBER						
Sun.	Mon.	Tues.	Wed.	Thur.	Fri.	Sat.
•	1	2	3	4	5	6
7	8	9	10	11	12	13
14	15	16	17	18	19	20
21	22	23	24	25	26	27
28	29	30	31	•	•	•

8.6 On arrival at their destination, evacuees and host families had to be introduced, and WVS co-operated with billeting officers to smooth out difficulties.
(WVS calendar)

When gifts of clothing from the USA and the Dominions began to arrive, the WVS was called upon to arrange for the distribution. After the advent of clothing rationing, they set up Clothing Exchange Centres, mainly for children's clothing. No money was involved and a points system was established.

Employers were required to provide canteen facilities but many new factories had to go into production before canteen facilities could be set up. To overcome their problem, the WVS ran mobile canteens and provided cooked meals for both day and night shifts.

As shortages of raw materials became more critical, they added salvage of any re-usable materials to their aluminium collection, with paper, bones and rags being collected.

They "went netting" – camouflage nets – which was a dirty, disagreeable job. All over the country net frames were set up in village halls, barns or any large enough building available. The WVS his-

torian describes how 'the dust and fluff from the scrim half choked the women knotting it onto the nets, and the dye left their hands and clothes deeply stained. Crawling about . . . with bruised knees and aching backs, elderly women drove themselves on for that extra hour which meant so many more square feet of cover for the British Army,' and a regular "netter" says, 'We wore overalls, a scarf round our hair and a mask something like a surgical mask.'

Towards the end of the war, preparations were made to provide large numbers of garments for the occupied countries, particularly for children. There was a lack of factory capacity to manufacture them, so the Ministry of Supply asked voluntary organisations to make them. When the invasion of Europe began, it was clear that the plight of the children was far worse than had been anticipated and the WVS increased their target for knitting from five tons to 10 tons per month. This was a super-human task, in a country already

KNITTING LEAFLET No. 1

CLOTHING FOR LIBERATED EUROPE

● **COATS FOR CHILDREN UNDER TWO**

Fig. A.

COAT (Boy or Girl) Fifteen months to two years. Fig. A.

MATERIALS:—5 oz. Wool. Two No. 9 Needles. Three Buttons.
MEASUREMENTS:—Length, 14 ins. Width, 23 ins. Length of sleeve (cuff turned up), 9 ins.
TENSION:—7 stitches to inch in width.
Commencing at lower edge of Right Front, cast on 50 stitches.
1st row.—K.1, (K.4, P.4) six times, K.1.
Repeat this row five times.
7th row.—K.1, (P.4, K.4) nine times, K.1.
Repeat 7th row five times.
13th row.—K.5, P.4, knit to end of row.
14th row.—K.1, purl to last 9 sts., K.4, P.4, K.1.
Repeat 13th and 14th rows twice.
Keeping a border of 2 blocks at front edge, work 26 rows without shaping.
In next row K.1, P.2, P.2 together, wool over needle (for button-hole), knit to end of row.

Still keeping border at front edge, continue without shaping, making a button-hole as before in every following 36th row until there are three button-holes in all.
Work 3 rows without shaping.
Cast off 16 sts. at beginning of next row.
Work one row without shaping.
Decrease once at neck edge in every row until 26 sts. remain.
Work 6 rows without shaping. Leave until Left Front has been worked.
Work Left Front to correspond with Right Front, including button-holes and ending with a purl row.

1   P.T.O.

KNITTING LEAFLET No. 2

CLOTHING FOR LIBERATED EUROPE

● **CARDIGANS FOR CHILDREN UNDER TEN**

Fig. A.

CARDIGAN (Boy or Girl) Two to four years. Fig. A.

MATERIALS:—4 oz. Wool. Two No. 9 Needles. Four Buttons.
MEASUREMENTS:—Length, 13 ins. Width, 24 ins. Length of sleeve, 10 ins.
TENSION:—7 stitches to inch in width.
Commencing at lower edge of Back, cast on 80 stitches. Work 6 rows in (K.1, P.1) rib.
7th row.—Knit. **8th row.**—Purl. Repeat 7th and 8th rows fifty-two times.
113th row.—K.29, (K.2 together, K.8) twice, K.2 tog., K.29.
114th row.—K.1, P.22, (K.1, P.1) fifteen times, K.1, P.22, K.1.
115th row.—K.23, (P.1, K.1) fifteen times, P.1, K.23.
Repeat 114th and 115th rows twice.
120th row.—K.1, P.21, (P.1, K.1) four times, cast off 17 sts., (K.1, P.1) four times, P.21, K.1.
Work 8 rows without shaping on last 30 sts., keeping a border of 8 sts. in rib at neck edge. Proceed as follows:
1st row.—Knit to last 9 sts., increase once in next st., (K.1, P.1) three times, K.2.

2nd row.—(K.1, P.1) four times, purl to last st., K.1.
3rd row.—Knit to last 8 sts., (K.1, P.1) three times, K.2.
4th row.—(K.1, P.1) three times, K.1, increase once in next st. purlways, purl to last st., K.1.
5th row.—Knit to last 8 sts., (K.1, P.1) three times, K.2.
6th row.—(K.1, P.1) four times, purl to last st., K.1. Repeat from 1st to 6th row seven times (46 sts.).
In next row knit to last 7 sts., P.1, K.1, P.1, wool round needle, P.2 tog. (for button-hole), K.2.
Work without shaping, keeping 8 sts. in rib at front edge, making a button-hole as before in every following 20th row until there are three buttonholes in all. Work 17 rows without shaping.

1

Knitting leaflets for garments for the children in liberated Europe.

FEBRUARY						
Sun.	Mon.	Tues.	Wed.	Thur.	Fri.	Sat.
•	•	•	•	1	2	3
4	5	6	7	8	9	10
11	12	13	14	15	16	17
18	19	20	21	22	23	24
25	26	27	28	•	•	•

After an air raid the WVS was on hand to help injured and bombed-out to find relations, and somewhere to sleep if necessary and to answer queries and give comfort.
(WVS calendar)

MARCH						
Sun.	Mon.	Tues.	Wed.	Thur.	Fri.	Sat.
•	•	•	•	1	2	3
4	5	6	7	8	9	10
11	12	13	14	15	16	17
18	19	20	21	22	23	24
25	26	27	28	29	30	31

Those who had lost their homes in air raids needed clothing, etc. as well as comfort and reassurance – WVS Clothing Centres fulfilled this need.
(WVS calendar)

seemingly stretched to the limits, coping with their own lives, as well as feeling inexpressibly weary after five years of war.

For women who could spare little time from household duties, there was the Housewives Service which aimed to ensure that there were one or two women in each street who would act as a steadying influence and provide elementary first aid should the need arise. It was of particular value during the air raids, when they could keep an eye on the needs of their immediate neighbourhood. They could take such action as sweeping broken glass off roads and pavements. This prevented punctures and damage to shoes and feet. The motto of the Housewives Service was 'A little thing is but a little thing but faithfulness in little things is a very great thing', a quotation from *St Augustine*.

It was perhaps in the air raids that the WVS felt that it was really fulfilling the purpose for which it had been set up, and its members excelled themselves in dealing with each crisis as it confronted them. They set up Incident Enquiry Posts where there was a bad centre of damage. It could be harrowing work, identifying casualties, helping distraught enquirers to find their relations, dealing with the shocked survivors, before moving on to start all over again at a new "incident".

To give one example out of countless numbers, the Centre Organiser in Bermondsey organised a

convoy of vehicles to evacuate people from shelters between spreading fires and the river. She was warned of the dangers, as the two bridges were near petrol sources and gas works threatened by fires, but she ignored the warnings and led whatever vehicles she could muster over the river. She succeeded in evacuating all the old people and expectant mothers from the area. The next morning, one bridge was blocked by an unexploded bomb and the other had holes in its structure, but the WVS organiser was determined to get canteens to the docks for civil defence workers and firemen.

REST CENTRE

APRIL						
Sun.	Mon.	Tues.	Wed.	Thur.	Fri.	Sat.
1	2	3	4	5	6	7
8	9	10	11	12	13	14
15	16	17	18	19	20	21
22	23	24	25	26	27	28
29	30	·	·	·	·	·

Rest Centres staffed by WVS

(WVS calendar)

She took the vehicles over planks laid across the holes. Charles Graves says, in *Women in Green*, 'What she had done, and so many members of the WVS were destined to do after her was to show how important to the struggle were the efforts of individual women.'

Lady Reading's message in June 1945 summarises the service the WVS rendered to the country. She referred to the 'seven years since WVS was started – which to most of us seemed like seven centuries . . . We have learned that it is no good talking about things, we must do them, and . . . to do that we must take pains, dislocate our lives and our comfort . . . We have done work we had never thought to approach and we have carried burdens heavier than we knew existed . . . We now know that in life no obstacle can block, it can only impede; that tiredness is an incident, not a finality.'

The WVS provide vegetables with all-important vitamins to the Navy
(WVS calendar)

The remains of a wrecked canteen which was previously staffed by the WVS
(WVS calendar)

Citizens' Advice Bureaux

It was anticipated that wartime would involve such widespread changes in living conditions, and such an avalanche of Government directives, restrictions, etc., that some central channel must be instituted to disseminate all information as quickly and accurately as possible and to be in a position to offer advice and clarification.

In 1938, the National Council of Social Service discussed with various national voluntary organisations the way such a service could be set up and it was decided that arrangements must be put in train for the setting up of local centres to which everyone could turn, and which would be equipped as far as possible to answer all queries or be in a position to direct the enquirer to the places where their problems could be dealt with.

Several national and local voluntary organisations co-operated with the establishment of such offices, and thus the Citizens' Advice Bureaux came into being as soon as war was declared. At first they were mainly under the wing of established organisations – Social Service departments, in one Yorkshire town Toc H, in the Midlands a Rotary Club, in another town the Soroptomists Club – and the premises were frequently makeshift, in rooms loaned by clubs, churches, youth centres or local councils.

The National Council of Social Service provided a headquarters, where a steady flow of reliable information could be collected, duplicated and channelled to the bureaux. The staff was mainly voluntary and usually part-time, sometimes having had social work or professional training. They came from all walks of life; most important was the ability to relate their training and experience to whatever problems arose. In the course of the war over 1,000 bureaux were set up and the vast majority of the 10,000 staff were women.

In the air raids, they manned desks in every information centre, and also manned mobile units to go to the worst hit areas. At the time of the flying bombs and rockets raids on London, teams came in from all parts of the country to help – under these conditions it was not practicable to set up fixed centres and a variety of vehicles were pressed into service. The first was a van loaned by the Friends' Ambulance Unit. This was followed by such diverse vehicles as a double-decker bus, a horsebox and even a private car carrying tents and camp beds for the staff. Most Civil Defence areas

War time: Horse box used as mobile CAB

(From CAB Collection *Photo: Bath & Wilts Evening Chronicle*)

had one or two "mobiles" of some sort available and teams prepared to take them wherever they might be needed.

Local bureaux were in close touch with the local offices of Government departments, plus those of the local authorities and with any voluntary organisations in their district. Through their close contact with individuals, they helped to streamline many Government schemes by being able to indicate where difficulties and delays were greatest. It was soon recognised that the CAB never regarded a problem as totally insoluble.

The service had to be adaptable and flexible, capable of adjusting to the rapid changes in social life brought about by the war, and the way the women in the first bureaux, working with few guidelines, in circumstances with no precedent, built up a reputation for reliability — almost of infallibility, earning the trust of all classes is emphasised by the fact that its value was recognised in matters not directly attributable to the war, so that when peace came, there was no question of closing such a widely used and universally highly regarded organisation.

If You Want To Know Ask the CAB (They Answer 10,000 Queries a Month)

The answer to 'If you want to know the time' may still be 'Ask a policeman' — though the GPO would say it was 'Ring the talking clock' — but the wise person will take most other wartime queries to the see-ay-bee (standing for CAB, the Citizens Advice Bureau).

Next week the CAB, the encyclopaedia of war information in the South-west, is taking a deep breath and, for once, talking about itself. It is not doing so out of self-pride; though it would be very justified in being self-congratulatory about the great amount of worry it lifts from the shoulders of thousands of citizens. No; it is running a campaign to publicise itself, because although so many people go for advice to its offices, all over the regions, it thinks that there are many more who do not realise what service the CAB puts at their disposal.

Here is the record of the CAB in the South-west during one month: Ten thousand enquiries answered; 1,500 rationing problems dealt with; 100 worries settled for relatives of prisoners of war; 500 queries solved about evacuees and billeting; expert and kindly advice given on 350 family and matrimonial problems.

That is a record of which the CAB in the South-west can be proud. It says nothing of the hundreds of inquiries about other topics, such as employment, family and service allowances, insurance and pensions, income tax and price complaints.

The CAB is a voluntary movement, run almost entirely by voluntary workers and largely financed by voluntary funds. It works in close co-operation with the Government and with local bodies.

Recently in the South-west it helped to find over a dozen anxious relatives of men and women who had been trapped by the Japanese advance in the Far East. It was able to tell them their friends were safe and on their way back to this country. This heart-easing work was just a part of its full service — done with the co-operation of Government departments and of local newspapers, who told their readers that such advice was waiting at local offices of the CAB.

Newspaper report – 6th November 1942

Peace: The Queen (now the Queen Mother) leaving a London CAB   (From CAB Collection *Photo: Mitcham News & Mercury*)

Police

For some years before the war there had been considerable pressure on the police authority to appoint more policewomen, and various women's organisations and the Home Office felt that wartime conditions posed even more moral and social problems which women were particularly suited to cope with. There was resistance to the suggestion and, as time went on, the availability of suitable candidates decreased steadily as women were absorbed into other war work. When, in 1944, the Home Office again pressed for numbers to be increased, the pre-war figure of 200 policewomen had only been doubled.

Meanwhile, in 1939, the Home Office had set up the Women's Auxiliary Police Corps, to be paid on the same wage scale as Civil Defence workers. The members of this Corps were not to be used to undertake any of the duties of regular police-women, but were to take over such posts as clerks, telephonists and drivers which would release a number of men for the armed forces as well as for ordinary police duties.

By 1941 there were about 200 full-time and 400 part-time WAPCs and, because of the increasing pressures on the regular force, some 60–70 of these had been attested and were assisting regular policewomen.

Numbers increased steadily and by 1945 there were 3,500 WAPCs on full-time duty, and perhaps 500 of these had been attested and were employed on regular police duties. Through the work of the WAPCs the very real contribution that women could make was established, and though their wartime story is not spectacular, the WAPC filled a role which was progressively more appreciated. They laid the foundations for the present incorporation of women in the Police Force.

A smartly uniformed member of Peterborough City Force in 1944.

Left –WAPC Audry Tee, Joined 6 October 1943, left 4 February 1946.

(Photo: Leicester City Police)

WPC Carnegie-Brown (centre) Joined 1921, promoted Sergeant 1941

(Photo: Picture Post)

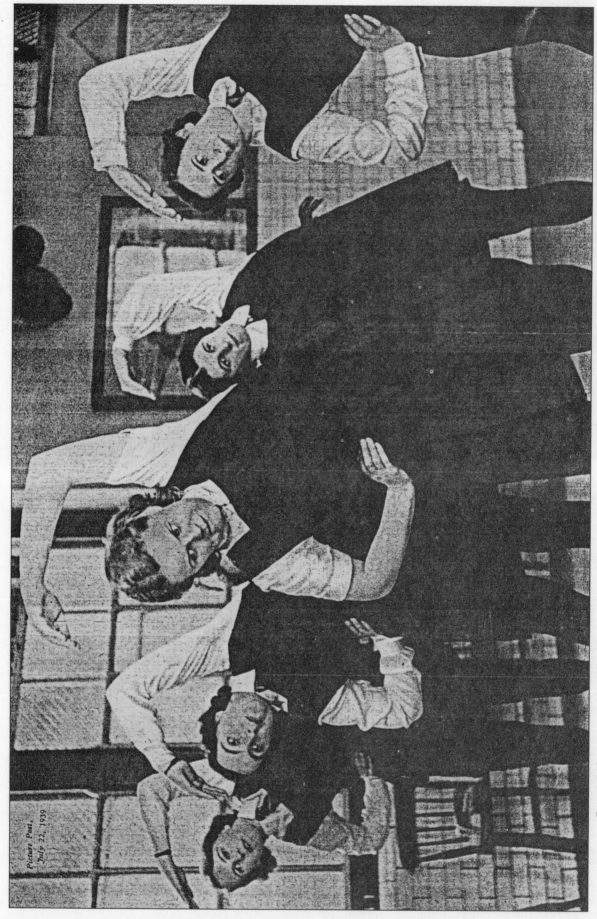

Picture Post,
July 22, 1939

Future Policewomen in the gym c. 1939. Physical training was important. Three time a week, candidates had classes. They did not go in for strenuous gymnastics. Keep fit on simple Swedish drill. They wore grey tunics, blouses and long black stockings.

(Photo: Picture Post)

Left – Parade for duty – before starting the day's work the new policewoman parades for duty in the station yard with her colleagues. The inspector reads out the day's instructions.
(Photo: Picture Post)

Right – Taking a call at a Police Box – She is being called from the station. She may be wanted to deal with a stranded girl, to take charge of an attempted suicide, or to bring back a woman prisoner.
(Photo: Picture Post)

Below – The sergeant shows the new recruit the beat which she will soon be responsible for herself. She's started out on her new carrer, a career full of responsibility and full of interest.
(Photo: Picture Post)

Fitting out a new batch of recruits – A small room with honeycombed walls, full of boots and shoes and stockings. There are piles of tacked-up suits and a long bench for cutting. It's a fitting room, where women police are measured and fitted out.
(Photo: Picture Post)

Women's Institutes

In retrospect, it seems surprising that the Women's Institute decided at the outset of the war that their participation in war work should be severely restricted 'out of respect for the beliefs of Quaker members'. This over-sensitive decision cost the WI a large number of members – there was a fall from 332,000 in 1939 to 288,000 in 1942, though after that numbers began to recover slowly.

However, in spite of this restrictive stance, the WI managed to make very valuable contributions in several fields. The WI had, in fact, evacuation and billeting plans in preparation well before the outbreak of war. Although these plans were superseded by those of the WVS, the village Institutes still played a large part in the reception and settlement of the evacuees when they arrived. In many areas they set up knitting and sewing circles to cope with the needs of the children, particularly necessary for those youngsters who came from poor city areas.

Lectures and day schools were geared towards "make do and mend", cooking with rationed foods, general shortages, do-it-yourself domestic repairs and any other skills which would ease home conditions.

Food production came high on their list of priorities. WI markets had been well established before 1939 and they were expanded rapidly,

being set up in villages as well as in the towns where they had initially been sited.

A comprehensive scheme was set in motion to distribute fruit bushes and vegetable seeds. Through the Institutes 140,000 bushes and 134,000 packets of seeds were sold, in addition to the circulation of large gifts of seed from overseas.

The WIs ran the majority of collecting centres for rose hips and herbs. From 1941 rosehip syrup became a familiar substitute for orange juice in Welfare Centres.

Fruit Preservation Centre – *The History of the Women's Institute Movement*

Their best known activity was jam making. The WI may be currently talking about getting away from their "jam and Jerusalem" image, but there were many people during the war who were grateful for the WI jam which was preferable to the factory produce. Because of sugar rationing there was little home jam making and preserving so, to utilise the surplus fruit, the Government provided much of the equipment and the sugar; implementing strict regulations about quality control. By the end of the scheme, over 5,300 tons had been made. Five hundred canning machines, sent as a gift from the women of America, were used to full capacity.

Though complete co-operation with wartime organisations was proscribed, the WI fully participated in any activity which could be regarded as necessary for the well-being of the civilian population.

WORK OF THE WOMEN'S INSTITUTE APPRECIATED

Message of Thanks from The Minister of Food

The Wiltshire Federation of Women's Institutes has received an appreciative letter from Lord Woolton (Minister of Food) thanking the members for their work of fruit preservation.

The Agricultural Sub-committee under the Chairmanship of Mrs C. W. Whatley was directly responsible for carrying out the scheme. The work was undertaken at 66 different Centres in the county by members of the WI and many other willing helpers.

As a result of this entirely voluntary effort, 19 tons of the fruit crop was saved; approximately 29 tons of jam being made; this figure does not include jellies, bottled and canned fruits, etc. The Federation have again been asked by the Ministry of Food to undertake this work for the coming season.

The letter sent to Lady Denman, of the National Federation of Women's Institutes, was as follows: 'I have just seen your Agricultural Organiser's report on the results of the co-operative fruit preservation scheme which was carried out last summer at 2,600 centres set up and managed by your Institutes.

'I have been very greatly impressed both by the quantity of preserves made and by the enthusiasm and determination with which the members of these centres, whether they belonged to your Institutes or not undertook the formidable task of saving the exceptionally heavy plum crop, as well as other garden and wild fruit. This was work of national importance demanding administrative ability of a high order at the Headquarters of your organisation, and local initiative and co-operation which are a fine example of democratic action at its best.

'I know also that the centres are eager to extend and improve upon their performance in 1941. I should be glad if you would pass on to them this message of thanks for the good work done last season and of encouragement to prepare now for the even greater effort which I hope will be possible this year.'

Newspaper cutting – 14th February 1941

The Rural Meat Pie scheme in operation near Reading, Berkshire.
(Photo: Cameron Books & The University of Reading)

Townswomen's Guild

The Townswomen's Guild was founded in 1929 and, when war was declared, it was a small and not at all wealthy organisation. In the event of war, they saw no specific role for the TWG and it was decided to suspend their activities for the duration. When war was declared, all the Headquarters' staff was dismissed, apart from Alice Franklin who volunteered to keep the organisation "ticking over" singlehanded.

However, the guilds had other ideas. Money and encouragement came in from all over the country. In October 1939 a small skeleton staff was re-engaged and TWG activities recommenced.

Of course, under wartime conditions there was always work waiting to be undertaken and the Townswomen's Guilds rapidly found spheres in which they could offer valuable service.

With the appeal to "dig for victory" and produce more vegetables, many parks were dug for use as allotments, and in many towns the TWG took responsibility for these projects.

Although they did not have such easy access to the countryside as the Women's Institutes, they also took part in the collection of herbs. One plant not scarce in urban areas was the stinging nettle and large quantities were gathered. The *History of*

The TWG mentions a "nettle party" arranged by Rosehill and Willington TG. It notes: 'It was a most enjoyable afternoon, and 17lb. of nettles were handed in to the drying centre at Newcastle.'

At Guildford there was a collecting centre which was open daily to receive nettles, foxglove seeds, rosehips and horse chestnuts. Sphagnum moss was also collected for use in hospitals.

Where suitable fruit was available, the TWG also undertook some jam making, though it is the Women's Institute chiefly remembered for this activity.

As man-power became more and more stretched, part-time workers for shops and offices played an increasingly important role, and the guilds began keeping registers of available workers. They organised recruiting centres for part-timers and the Ministry of Labour recognised these centres as official bureaux for part-time work.

In reception areas they were able to provide social centres for evacuees and club rooms where visiting parents could spend weekend visits.

In spite of an uncertain start, the Townswomen's Guilds had found a number of niches in which they were able to make a noteworthy contribution to the war effort.

Townswomen's Guild members running a makeshift canteen, 1945.

Blue Cross

Thought was given to the welfare of animals as well as humans — starting in Glasgow and west Scotland, ARP animal wardens were appointed, and throughout the country the number rose to over 1,500. Their main duty was to guard against panic at stock markets, particularly in urban areas, and to tag and register farm animals so that in the event of enemy action, straying animals could be identified. A good deal of the latter work was carried out by women, but this registration came to be regarded as overly cautious and the practice was allowed to die out.

"Our Dumb Friends League" carried on work which they had started in the 1914—18 war and made provisions for pets — primarily dogs and cats — of servicemen. Many members of the forces, when they were called up, left behind dogs who could not be cared for at home — particularly in the cities. Young wives might be evacuated and those who remained might be working very long hours and sleeping in communal air raid shelters at night. Boarding kennels were opened where such pets would be accommodated free and their owners could visit them when they were on leave and, if it was convenient, take them home for a while.

The demand for this service soon outstripped the supply and appeals were made for "billets" to accommodate the "evacuees".

In the boarding kennels, women undertook most of the organisation and the kennel work, earning the heartfelt thanks of many soldiers, sailors and airmen whose pets might well have had to be put down without this canine evacuation scheme.

Illustrations from a leaflet about boarding kennels — 'There are many sad partings as well as happy reunions, but at least the service men's dogs are safe with us.'

In 1939 there were comparatively few women employed in industry, and those were mainly in light and unskilled work. By the time of peak wartime production there were about three women to every five men. The Government statistics are a little misleading. Those issued in 1944 show the number of women in industry as 1,851,000 (compared to 506,000 in 1939) but the true figure was probably over 2,000,000 because part-time women workers were only counted as half a worker in official calculations.

At first, employers tended to have doubts about the capacity of women to cope with heavy machinery or highly technical operations. There was a fairly widespread resistance to starting training schemes for them. So, a network of Government Training Centres was set up throughout the country where the basic skills could be learned and, in some cases, the women's first awe of machinery could be overcome before they started work on the factory floor. Little training was needed to operate the comparatively simple machines which stamped out small aluminium parts for aircraft engines but it was not long before women were working to limits of finer than 0.00025" on optical grinding and polishing.

The work was very varied. The name "munitions factory" called up a picture of a fairly grim job. Veena Moore certainly expected this when she was called up. She had a choice of the forces or munitions and she says she chose the latter mainly because she thought the forces' medicals would involve a dental inspection. She said, 'I was scared stiff after having had very painful sessions at the dentist's.' So, munitions it had to be, and she was determined to be prepared. She said, 'I bought

THEY WEAR "RAISE THE STANDARD" SMILES

May Wheeler went to live with her aunt in Dumfries after heavy raids on her home town of Greenock. She found work in a munitions factory in an isolated spot on the Solway Firth. She says, 'My job was baling the gun cotton and making cordite. Handling cordite was a very dangerous job but I earned good money. £18 a week in those days was a lot. We had special clothing to wear and we were searched every time we clocked in for hair grips or any other metal which could cause a spark and possible disaster.' After May married, her husband was posted south, so she moved too, to Folkestone. She found a job quite easily, making ammunition boxes but at much reduced pay. Her wages were then 11d. (5p) an hour. The photograph above shows May and her colleagues. The photograph shows the special clothing supplied to the girls working with explosives – felt boots, grey flannel trousers and a navy blue top with a light blue band across. The clothes were kept in lockers at the factory and changed twice a week. May Wheeler is second from the left.

REME Workshops.

Kathleen Maslin's father was an inspector in the REME workshops in Warminster, and when the skilled mechanics were posted overseas, it was suggested that women should take their place. Kathleen had worked as a machinist in a glove factory before the war, so she was used to using her hands and she and other local women went into the workshops and within a year were able to overhaul Brenn carriers without help, apart from supervision from their instructors. 'They take a little longer than the men', said the colonel, 'but their work is perfect.'

Kathleen began by going to a Government Training Centre for three months, which she did not find had much reference to he subsequent work in the REME workshops! With the training she received in the workshops she was able within a few months to take out the engine from a tank and replace it with a new one.

The girls worked from 7.30 to 5.45 every day; two nights a week they worked on to 7.45 but finished at 12.30 on Saturday. They had a canteen which provided a hot meal every day and also tea and sandwiches.

REME Workshops.   *(Photo: Woman Magazine)*

Amy Beattie went into Rutherford's ship repair yard in Liverpool in 1943 and stayed until it closed in 1962! When she started most of the women were doing fairly light work but she was put into the blacksmith's shop as a steam hammer driver. The other women in the works finished in 1945 but her boss would not let her go.

clothing coupons on the black market, bought two pairs of dungarees and set off for what I thought was going to be a dirty, greasy job.' In fact, she was sent to Smith's watch factory at Cheltenham and trained as a jewel setter. She had to learn to use an eye-glass and to handle jewels no bigger than a grain of sugar, in a dust free, highly polished workshop. Her first introduction to the jewels was not immediately successful. 'I sat looking across the lovely countryside, leaning on my desk, not realising that the jewels had been laid out with the other equipment. But they weren't on the desk, because they were sticking up the sides of my arms, while I was busy mastering the art of keeping my eye- glass in position and handling the tweezers. A good laugh was had by all – and, incidentally, I didn't require the overalls.' She soon came to terms with the work and stayed at Smith's for some time.

At the other end of the scale, in the heavy iron and steel industry, women were doing over 900 different jobs. They worked as steel smelters and iron puddlers, they drove the overhead cranes carrying molten metal from furnace to moulding sheds. All work which would have been unthinkable for women a few years earlier.

Veena Moore, who expected a factory job to be heavy and dirty but worked on fine precision instruments.

Irene Hill of Bridport was a sheet metal worker for the British Power Boat Company at Hythe, making motor torpedo boats and sea rescue craft for airmen. She trained for two months at Marchwood before going to work in the factory. Once trained it was quite a well-paid job. Her final pay packet contained £6. 11s. 8d. (£6.58). The photograph (right) shows Irene and colleagues on the training course at Marchwood.

Items prepared by women sheet metal workers for RAF rescue boats and gun craft included mouthpieces for speaking tubes, engine back rest clips, petrol drip trays, sliding door treads, conduct saddles, bonella lamp brackets, engine bed capping, exhaust plates, bot frame clips, tubular struts for wheelhouse, wardroom toilet trays, guards for choke fairleads, bulkhead petrol glands, gear oil tank pipes, galley fuse panels, self-bailer rose boxes, elbow covers and cradle straps.

Maureen Weinstock worked in a munitions factory outside Liverpool. For the first two years she was an assistant to an engineer whose work was establishing why some of the shells did not come up to the required standard. Later, Maureen was in charge of workshops filling landmines, bombs and rockets. It was responsible work requiring high technical ability. She says that she was one of a small number of women who became shop managers in this work.

Elsie Allen worked pre-war in a high-class milliner's in the West End of London. This was not essential wartime work so she answered an advertisement for 'women with nimble fingers and plenty of patience'. Having these qualifications, she joined the firm of Johnson Matthey where she worked for the duration of the war and many years afterwards. On retirement, an appreciation of her service in the firm's journal noted: 'The whole period of her 31 years of service has been devoted entirely to the production of diamond wire drawing dies in one form or another. Elsie's service started on 20th July 1940, when she joined Dr Chaston and Mr Ashby in the physics laboratory to set up with the help of BDWD (Dorset) a re-servicing unit for diamond dies. It was during the period of World War II, when Holland and France had collapsed, that the supply of new diamond dies to this country was halted and it became vital to the national effort that all existing diamond dies were maintained to give the best possible drawing life.' So Elsie Allen became the first diamond die polisher trained for Johnson Matthey, and it was from her efforts that today's Diamond Die Department has grown. Elsie's name can be linked with every stage of the diamond die re-servicing programme at Wembley, from small beginnings in the laboratory via the famous Wembley coaches, to the building of the new Die Department in 1949. Her sister who was in the WAAF adds that, 'the Wembley coaches were converted railway carriages, freezing in winter and boiling in summer. There were no commercial dies available at the time to clear the dies, and Elsie hit on the idea of using sewing needles but these, like so many other things, were in short supply. Elsie's relations and friends were directed to visit haberdashers and buy up all they could find.'

In the Wembley coaches. Elsie Allen is on the left in the front row.

WOMEN TO KEEP THE PHONE OPEN

Yet another way for service has been opened to West Country women by the Post Office.

Throughout the provinces 800 women, many of them in the West of England, are being sought to replace the men who used to work behind the scenes in the telephone exchange. Thousands of men have been called to join the Forces. Those who remain must be out in the streets and in the bomb craters repairing the cables.

So women are to be given the chance to show their engineering bent. Some will repair the cords, others wire up the huge distribution frames where the hundreds of telephone circuits are split up, while their comrades will check the circuits and the hundred and one vital details which go to make up the telephone system.

The employment of women for this class of work is definitely a war time emergency measure and will cease when hostilities come to an end.

But in the meantime absorbingly interesting work, in which they will be trained by Post Office engineers, is being thrown open to women, at rates of pay which range from 40s. to 15s.

Newspaper report – 7th February 1941

The type of multiple die wire drawing machine on which Elsie Allen worked. *(Photo: Johnson Matthey)*

In 1942, Clement Attlee, deputy to Winston Churchill, said, 'The work women are performing in munitions factories has to be seen to be believed. Precision engineering jobs which a few years ago would have made a skilled turner's hair stand on end, are being performed with dead accuracy by girls who have had no industrial experience.' High praise indeed; Clement Atlee did not pay compliments lightly.

Thelma Nevitt, at 19 years of age, answered an advertisement asking for women of School Certificate Standard and preferably those good at mathematics for 'very important work inspecting various parts of aeroplanes, also engines, wireless and electrical equipment, etc., to make sure that all such supplies, before delivery from the manufacturers' works, are safe in every way for use by the RAF.' Thelma, now living in Bournemouth, said, 'After an interview I was appointed to the Aero-Engine Division. Following my attendance at two very highly-concentrated courses in aeronautical engineering at a special Aeronautical Inspection Directorate training school, I was posted to Rolls-Royce, Crewe, where Merlin engines were produced. I eventually reached AID examiner status. I am very proud of the fact that I became one of the few AID women who had the capacity to supervise the bench testing of aero-engines and was able to check and certify the very complicated calculations relating to their performance under simulated flight conditions as carried out by Rolls-Royce's own test bed inspectors. After Final Test my signature testified for the AID that the engine was accepted and passed off – in other words, fit to enter the service of the Royal Air Force.'

In spite of the obvious need for ever-increasing numbers of munitions and heavy-industry workers, the trade unions were unwilling to accept women employees as members. In early 1940, Fred Smith of the AEU said, 'The AEU is, and always has been, opposed to the introduction of women into the engineering industry . . . Not with the consent of the Union would women be brought in in normal times.' Later the same year the Annual Conference voted against admitting them to the membership.

It was not until two years later that women were accepted as members of the AEU, and then the about-turn was complete. They were accorded complete equality with men – equal pay for equal work and parity in all aspects of union organisation.

Fortunately, conditions in the munitions factories were incomparably better than during the First World War when the workers suffered quite horribly and TNT poisoning was frequent. Physical strength and stamina were not as great in women as in men. The work added to the wartime stresses and shortages, causing some illness, but on the whole the health of women in industry was

Engine test bench cabin as used in the inspection of aero-engines. (A) Pressure gauge for petrol pump. (B) Oil scavenge pressure gauge. (C) Air speed indicator. (E) Watch. (F) Main oil pressure gauge. (G) Crankcase oil pressure gauge. (H) Air compressor gauge. (I) Transmitting type oil thermometers. (J) Flexible drive for Hasler. (K) Engine switches. (L) Tachometer two-way box. (M) Cold junction for thermo couples. (N) Galvanometer for recording temperatures. (O) Engine controls. (P) Thermo couple distribution box. (Q) Thermo couple leads.

better. The only exception was some small increase in anaemia and tuberculosis.

Marjorie Spreadbury wanted to go into the WAAF, but she was working in a balloon factory in Godalming and this was a reserved occupation. The factory made not only balloons, many for use on convoy ships, but also "decoy" lorries and landing craft, which she says looked very realistic when they were inflated, and inflatable rescue boats.

Marking up sheets of fabric for balloons. Marjorie says they seemed to need miles of fabric. 'Oh our poor knees did suffer!'

A shed of completed rescue boats in the balloon factory.

Marjorie Spreadbury marking heavy rubber sheet used in making "decoy" tanks and lorries.

Girls joining panels of silver fabric for convoy balloons which were used on ships.

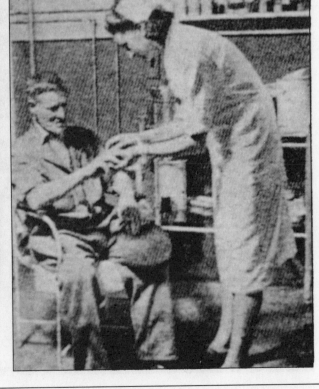

Every effort was made to make factory work easier for the workers — left, nurseries were provided for working mothers — right, well-equipped and staffed medical clinics were installed to deal with minor injuries.

(Photos: The War Illustrated)

Workers at Rest and Play

Top – Womens Work's Dart Championships – Going for the bull!

Middle – Queing to be served by the hard working canteen staff.

Bottom – 'Workers Playtime' – A lunchtime event in factories all over the country which were great morale boosters. Many of these performances were broadcast by the BBC.

Photos: British Official, Fox, Illustrated)

Transport

Not long after the outbreak of war, women began to appear in new roles in all branches of transport, on land and water. In July 1940, the first women were employed as conductors on London buses and within five years they had taken on 10,000. By 1944, Manchester was employing 1,800 women on buses and trams.

Helen Smith was one of the early "clippies" on London Transport. This was before it became necessary to direct women into the work. She had to undergo a tough medical and a general knowledge test, the same as the men. She had a grey uniform with blue bands on the cuffs and collar, but when women were directed onto the buses, standards were lowered somewhat and these conductors had a navy uniform with light blue bands. She says that when she was on a regular service with the same driver all the time she earned up to £8. 15s. 0d. (£8.75p) and thought she was a "millionaire", even though, if her money was short at the end of the day she had to make it up. The "clippies" got a lot of teasing and practical jokes from the men but on the whole there was a comradeship which made the work seem easier, even during the worst of the raids.

Not many women were trained as bus drivers. The first was probably Mrs Ellen Davies of Llantrisant, Gwent. London Transport employed some women on maintenance in the garages but only used them to drive empty buses and not on passenger services. There were more in Scotland and the North of England but it was still a negligible number.

In contrast, women replaced men in large numbers on goods vehicles, particularly on vans and lighter lorries. At least one city employed women to drive their dustcarts. Taxi driving was another sphere in which many women worked; some taking over when their husbands were called up.

On the railways, women quickly took a large part in keeping the services running. They worked as porters and delivered goods, plus fulfilling duties as guards and cleaners.

Helen Smith (second from left) was one of the early conductresses on London Transport. The uniform included divided skirts (now known as culottes) which were more seemly than ordinary skirts for running up and down stairs of the double-decker buses.

Sheila Court (pictured left in 1945) was directed during 1940 into work as a booking clerk and telegraphist at Heswall Hills station, in the Wirral. To work the telegraph system she had to learn Morse code, in which many of the messages were sent. Sheila had to de-code the messages before sending them on. Her work was very varied and wide-ranging. The goods yard served many British and American Army camps for which much equipment arrived by rail. There was also the usual civilian traffic and the yard was used by several coal merchants. All this had to be cleared and charges worked out on a daily basis for any goods remaining in the yard. There were many pigeon fanciers in the area, whose baskets were brought in early in the morning for weighing and despatch to other stations. Railway station staff were responsible for releasing the birds on their training flights. When the Station Master was not on duty, Sheila took full charge of Heswall Hills station plus a second station as well. She says that the most difficult part was trying to control two sixteen-year-old lad porters! She did not have a uniform, only a badge which allowed her to go to the front of bus queues in order to get to work on time.

Right — working on the permanent way.
(*Photo: British Railways Press*)

Below — caring for the cart horses. (*Photo: British Railways Press*)

Wyn Bowden was a guard in Devon. She was the daughter of a GWR railwayman and he helped her to take the necessary examination. The guard is in charge of the train, and she found that once she had shown she knew her job, the male drivers, firemen, etc. accepted her quite willingly. She remembers having her breakfast of sausages, bacon or eggs fried on the fireman's shovel and says it tasted fabulous.

Mrs Talbot's work was very different. She got a job as a cleaner and her husband says that when she got home after her first day's work, he hardly recognised her. He had imagined her sweeping the platforms on the underground, but in fact she was working on steam engines, cleaning smoke tubes, etc. By the end of the day, with the effects of the weather and soot, and only soft soap to wash with, her face was bright red, with white rings round her eyes where she had worn goggles.

She and a friend were the first women to be employed on this work. They were filmed and photographed by the press who christened them "the choo-choo chars".

Over one-sixth of the staff of British railways were women, working on the permanent way and in all departments of maintenance, as well as clerical, booking office work, etc. One depot making concrete sleepers was staffed entirely by women. Most of the horses used for goods deliveries were cared for and driven by women. In fact, apart from train drivers and firemen, there were very few jobs which women did not undertake.

On the inland waterways women had always played a considerable part in operating canal boats. Traditionally it was a family affair, with the boats being both work-place and home. It was not until 1943 that labour shortages really began to

One of the "choo-choo chars" cleaning a boiler

(Photo: British Rail)

Marie Clark (top right and third from left in top row below)worked in the Redbridge Railway yards near Southampton. The Group of women employed there eventually took over most of the work of the yard, which was heavy and dirty.

(Photo: Southern Railway)

Verena Bagot, of Worcester, was one of about half a dozen women who drove 1,000 gallon petrol tankers. It was heavy work and long hours. During one week in September 1943 she drove 528 miles, transported 11,890 gallons of petrol, made 37 deliveries and worked 48 hours on the trot. She was probably the first woman to become an RAC qualified driving instructor. Apart from the period driving the tanker she was an instructor for 30 years from 1935. Above left and right: Verena with the petrol tanker she drove during the war.

be felt on the waterways and women were invited to volunteer for work on the boats.

It was a demanding job. The crews had to maintain as well as run the engines. They also had to open and close innumerable lock gates. A crew of three ran a pair of boats – the motor-driven narrow boat and the butty boat which was towed; a pleasant enough job in the summer but a gruelling slog in winter, with "home" a ten feet by six feet cabin.

In 1944 there were 11 crews carrying cargoes between London and Birmingham. More followed in the Leeds-Liverpool area but there were never many "Idle Women" (the nickname came from the IW – Inland Waterways – badges).

Even fewer in number were the women who worked on seagoing vessels. At the beginning of the war, one woman, Miss Victoria Drummond, was a qualified marine engineer working on board a British ship. The other women who were at sea were stewardesses and they continued with their normal duties under the much more stringent wartime conditions.

Miss Drummond was awarded the MBE in 1941 and the citation reads: 'The ship was attacked for 35 minutes by a bomber, when 400 miles from land, but by skilful handling many hits were avoided. When the alarm was sounded, Miss Drummond at once went below and took charge. The first salvo flung her against the levers and nearly stunned her. When everything had been done to increase the ship's speed she ordered the engineroom and stokehole staff out. After one attack the main injection pipe just above her head started a

joint and scalding steam rushed out. She nursed this vital pipe through the explosion of each salvo, easing down when the noise of the aircraft told her that bombs were about to fall, and afterwards increasing steam. Her conduct was an inspiration to the ship's company and her devotion to duty prevented more serious damage to the vessel.'

For this action she was also awarded Lloyd's Medal for Bravery at Sea. She was the first woman to win this award. Later, two stewardesses also received this award for caring for shipwrecked passengers, regardless of their own safety.

Citation order of Member of British Empire MBE, Miss V. A. Drummond, Second Engineer

The ship was attacked for 35 minutes by a bomber, while 400 miles from land. By skilful handling, hits were avoided. The enemy was forced to use up all his bombs and ammunition, and a great deal of his fuel. Three times he failed even to get into his bombing position.

Altthough much damage was done to the vessel, there would have been far more but for the seamanship of the Master, and the courage of the 2nd Engineer.

This Officer is the only British woman engineer holding the Ministry of Shipping's Certificate of Competency. At the time of the attack she was able to coax an additional 3½ knots from the engines, and this speed was still rising by the time the attack ceased. When the alarm sounded, she at once went below and took charge. The first Salvo flung her against the levers and nearly stunned her. She ordered the other Engineers to open up the fuel injectors, and herself increased the main throttle bit by bit. She then gave the engine-room and stoke-hold staff the order "Get out".

After one attack the main injection pipe just above her head started a joint. Scalding steam rushed past her. She nursed this vital pipe through the explosion of each salvo, easing down when the noise of the aircraft engines told her that bombs were about to fall, holding on to a stanchion as they burst, and then increasing steam. The platform on which she stood was littered with bullets which came down through the skylight.

Within an hour of the attack this officer was again in her usual good spirits. Her whole conduct was an inspiration to the ship's company.

Inland Waterways employed a number of women crewing transport barges. Two run this boat alone carrying grain on Midlands Canals.

Meriol Trevor remembers her years on canal boats as a fascinating time in spite of the very heavy, dirty, sometimes dangerous work. She fell into the canal on three or four times, once dangerously near the propeller blades of a boat. There were no specific hours and work often went on as long as it was light. Pay was on a piecework basis but there was a guaranteed £3 per week. Canal boat crews didn't load or unload. Meriol remembers that the dockers threw the cargoes aboard anyhow which meant that the boats lay all ways in the water. The crew had to "sheet up" (pull the heavy tarpaulins over the uprights and make them fast with tarry rope). She recalls many quite frightening and unpleasant things such as meeting other boats in tunnels, getting ropes caught in propeller blades, water leaking into bedding and bugs in the boats, but she says she wouldn't have missed the experience for anything.

Above and left – Despite the bombing the 'clippie' was a familiar figure.

Below – The Girls – Engine cleaning.   *(Photo: L.M.S)*

Agriculture and Women's Land Army

The Women's Land Army, like many other women's services, came into being in the 1914—18 war. It was not started until 1917 and, like other organisations, was disbanded when the war ended. As with ATS, WAAFs and WRNs, the memory of the service and its value in wartime was kept alive among the women who had served in it.

The second phase sprang into life before the Second World War started. It was reformed in June 1939, though not on a full-time basis. Volunteers were registered and many spent their holidays at training camps so that when the war started, there were a thousand volunteers, many of whom had a little rudimentary training ready to go immediately into full-time employment.

By the end of 1939 there were 4,500 Land Girls working, and by 1943 there were 71,000. New recruits were given a month's introductory training and then a large number were placed as individual workers, either living on the farms or in lodgings nearby. By 1944 there were nearly 700 hostels, mainly run by the WLA, but including about 100 run by the YMCA and 75 by War Agricultural Executive Committees, accommodating over 22,000. Gangs from these camps moved from farm to farm for seasonal work, haymaking, potato picking, etc. and taking threshing machines round the farms in the various districts. Some women drove tractors on hire to farmers for ploughing and other cultivations.

Again taking 1943 figures, between ten and eleven thousand women were engaged in horticulture and in this field, which did not depend as much on physical strength and stamina as agriculture, the relative output of women as against men was often higher than that of the men they replaced. A relative output study carried out by the University of Wales showed that in agriculture, only in poultry work did women equal or exceed men's output, while in some jobs, notably muck-spreading and loading, the percentage was as low as 50 per cent. In planting, picking peas, beans, fruit, etc. the output was 95 per cent to 106 per cent that of men.

Apart from the obvious range of work, there was a number of more unusual jobs which were successfully undertaken by Land Girls. The craft of thatching was learned by gangs producing a sort of thatching "mat" and setting them on ricks.

H.M. Queen Elizabeth presenting service arm-bands to members of WLA Windsor Great Park 1943.

(Photo: Central Press Photos Ltd.)

Presentation of service arm bands in Windsor Great Park 1943. The two Princesses enjoy the occasion.   (*Photo: Central Press*)

Above — Campden WLA and Mrs Lane 'Wings for Victory' Parade, September 1943.
Left — Four smart girls after the presentation of medals at Worcester.   (*Photo: Brendan Kerney*)

After some time on fieldwork, going out to various farms in Cambridgeshire, Joan Thompson (above)transferred to the Plant Research Station in Cambridge. The main plant under research was the potato. Plants were grown both outdoors and in greenhouses. The boilers heating the greenhouses were coal-fired and had to be cleaned and stoked. The plants were watered by hand. Soil for the experiments had to be sterilised, as were the greenhouses which were regularly scrubbed. With few mechanical aids it was heavy work and necessitated time at weekends to maintain boilers and follow watering routines. Below: A parade of the Women's Land Army through Cambridge during July 1943. Joan is marked with a cross. Above:Joan Thompson in her Women's Land Army uniform, April 1943.

Mavis Drake (above) went into the Women's Land Army to work with animals but found herself potato picking. After potato picking came work with carrots (she says she still can't bear the sight of them) and then parsnips. No amount of tugging and pulling with broken fingernails would loosen the parsnips from the soil and they had to be dug up. Eventually, her wish was fulfilled, when she was sent to a dairy school. Mavis says, 'I shall never forget the first time I milked a cow. I remember feeling the warmth as I pushed my head into her hairy side, and the sound of the soft crunch of her munching hay plus the occasional low or belch. I also recall the sweet smell of the warm milk as it was squirted into the bucket. When I finished the cow looked round at me as if to say "not bad". Then she promptly had an "accident" down my milking smock.'

After a spell as a relief-milker, Mavis was eventually employed on a farm with a pedigree herd of Red Polls. She enjoyed learning about the importance of breed-lines, etc. but she had a *bete-noir* in the shape of 'an ancient, shaky, coke-fired monstrosity of a boiler' which was used to sterilise the milking equipment. She says, 'The old boiler would start thumping, the pipes did shake, the joints rattled and I would pray the needle would make haste so that I could quickly release the pressure and bring the whole lot back to its creaky normal condition.'

WLA Parade in Cambridge.

Winnie Weaver and her friend, Molly, went for two weeks' training as rodent exterminators at Appleby and worked in the Lake District, covering an area from Grasmere to Kendal. They used poison, traps and gas, visiting farms, hotels, cafes, a paper mill, sewage works and a Shorts' factory which made Sunderland flying boats. Winnie recalls how, strangely enough, they often found themselves on the side of the rats. Sometimes they would feed the rats with a non-poisonous substance for three days which made the rats tame enough to take food from a hand-help spoon. On the fourth day a lethal dose was administered via the spoon. Winnie said, 'You will understand that having gained the confidence of the rats, we shed tears for them on the fourth day.'

Molly, Vera and Ellen with dead rats at Appleby, 1941.

Winnie with rats caught at Low Fairbank.

In land drainage, women learned to operate grabs and excavators; they also dug ditches and laid tile drains. Much work was done in the Fens, on Wragmire Moss in Cumberland and on the River Skerne in Durham. The Thames Conservancy Board had a gang of Land Girls operating throughout the war.

Nearly a thousand Land Girls were employed by county councils in the war which goes on endlessly against rats. There were, and as far as I know there still are, more rats than people in this country, and the amount of food lost to them is tremendous. Rodent control is not a pleasant job. The way women got stuck into the job and their efficiency caused great surprise to the farmers they worked for.

There were, of course, many women already employed in agriculture, and even more in horticulture. Their numbers increased steadily. There were probably over twice as many employed privately in 1944 as at the beginning of the war. Women had always been employed locally on seasonal work – potato picking, hoeing, fruit picking, etc. – and with increasing food production, this was an ever-growing need. Large numbers of office workers, shop assistants, etc. spent their holidays in harvest camps.

At the beginning of the war, members of the Land Army could be employed in private gardens, provided these were primarily used for food production. Since farmers were at first somewhat suspicious of employing women, particularly as so many of the volunteers came from offices or "luxury" jobs in towns, and there had not so far been any great loss of men from farm work, the flood of volunteers easily met or even exceeded the demand. A year later this situation was reversed. Demand was growing rapidly and WLA members were no longer allocated to private gardens.

Here the Women's Farm and Garden Association was able to fill a valuable role. This association had been founded in 1899 to look after the interests of women who wished to work in agriculture or horticulture. It was dedicated to ensuring that good practical training was available and that women's standing in this field was upheld. Unfortunately, in the run up to the war, the Council of Management, though dedicated and able, took a rather elitist stand. They felt, perhaps understandably, that a huge influx of untrained volunteers, however enthusiastic, and however urgently needed, would detract from the image of a skilled female workforce which they had worked so long to establish. Consequently, there was virtually no co-operation or contact between WFGA and WLA, probably to the disadvantage of both. However, in large private gardens, in nurseries and on farms, the WFGA continued to give skilled and dedicated service.

Farmers' wives and families also took on more and more work on the farms. They had always played an active part but broadened their scope as occasion demanded. When Olive Stokes was 12 years old, her father linked three mowers behind a Fordson tractor, one tractor-drawn and two older horse-drawn machines. She and her mother

A slight lapse, a mix up of stool and bucket. Too early in the morning!

Try to get the food in the trough.

The duck that won't go to bed when it's your evening off.

It's not wise to turn your back on a playful bull!

Those pilots training – no thought for us loading hay.

After unloading the muck, Violet is keen to go home.

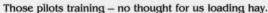

Dorothy Dennis cartoons

Dorothy Dennis went on a three-week training course, after which she worked on farms in Northamptonshire, Buckinghamshire and Wiltshire, milking, driving tractors and general farm work and recorded some of the impressions in pen and ink drawings.

manned the mowers while her 10–year-old brother drove the tractor. They not only cut the fields on their own farm at Margaret's Marsh near Shaftesbury but the children were allowed time off school and Violet Stokes took her small gang to mow for neighbouring farmers as well.

The WLA did not function as a totally non-skilled labour force. There were correspondence courses available, plus foremen's course, and proficiency tests could be taken in many subjects. A large number of Land Girls studied the theoretical as well as the practical side of their work. Many did not return to their town lives after the war.

The emergency did not end on the land with the cessation of hostilities. The food supply was still a matter of urgency and the WLA was not finally disbanded until November 1950, although numbers had dwindled steadily.

Pay and holidays were on a par with the Wages Orders of the Agricultural Wages Board, but for Land Girls there was a minimum laid down, after cost of board and lodgings had been taken into account. In 1943 this was 22s. 6d.

(£1.12½p) for a 48 hour week (50 hours in summer) or 18s. (90p) for 17–year-olds. Uniform, which is too well known to need description, was supplied free.

It was hoped that the WLA would be one of the services entitled to post-war gratuities and educational or training grants but Parliament decided to classify it as industrial and not as a wartime service. Lady Denman was so incensed at this decision that she resigned as the Director of the WLA in protest.

The WLA was not a spectacular form of service. There was more drudgery than glamour about the work. A few girls, mainly in the south and south-eastern counties, worked in some danger. A small number were killed or wounded in German air attacks but this was the exception. On the whole it was a life of slogging hard work, totally divorced from the previous experience of the shop assistants, typists, hairdressers, etc. who had joined, but it was of incalculable value in maintaining the home-grown food production, and, in fact, increased all agricultural and horticultural output.

Nan Kendall wanted to make horticulture her war work. She felt that the Women's Farm and Garden Association would give her a better training and more freedom of movement than the Women's Land Army. When she enrolled she went to Woodyates Manor for six weeks' basic training, doing practical work during the day and attending lectures in the evening. Following a simple written test she went on to do a six months' apprenticeship at Boyton Manor in Wiltshire, under the head gardener, Mr Company. Apprenticeship over, she went to Manor Farm at Teffont but found the agricultural work there much rougher than the horticultural skills she had learned. From Teffont she moved on to Baverstock Manor gardens, where she was in sole charge. This was a tribute to her training and work, which gave Mr Company considerable satisfaction. The work gave her pleasure and also contributed to the fresh food supply. The photograph shows a harvesting scene at Teffont.

Voluntary Land Club

Marjorie Thompstone was a teacher and thus unable to undertake full time war work but she undertook the necessary training to become a Civil Nursing Reserve. She did general nursing duties at weekends. Being near to Manchester she expected an influx of casualties the day after the heavy air raid on the city. To her dismay she was sent to Casualty but then to her disgust she was sent off to a side room to make Christmas decorations (a job she hated). After an illness, which necessitated a rest from voluntary work for a while, she joined a local Voluntary Land Club. On Saturdays and Sundays 'a jolly party of young people' went out to farms 'in the back of a knacker's smelly van'. They 'manured, set and picked potatoes by the hundredweight, gathered stones from a field, made hay and stacked it and stooked corn in sheaves. The first row had fallen down by the time we looked back. In one week of my holidays, alone, I thinned a field of kale'.

Irene Lodge started her war work when she was very young. Her family lived at Margaret Marsh near Shaftesbury. Irene's father, John Stokes, fixed up three trailer-mowers behind a Fordson tractor, Mrs Stokes took her little team – Irene, then aged 12, and brother John, aged 10 (who drove the tractor) – to neighbouring farms as well as cutting their own hay. The children were allowed time off school and they cut hundreds of acres of grass for hay. The photographs on this page show Irene, John and Mrs Stokes in action.

Land reclamation work with the Thames Conservancy Board.

Peggy Few worked for 5 years on drainage work for the Thames Conservancy reclaiming arable land along the river, and in all parts of Berkshire. It was in August 1942, after a short training period at Hull, that she joined the first twelve WLA volunteers to begin work with the Conservancy, driving powerful tractor-excavator. Peggy Few — pictured here in the cab — was the last to leave this group.

Parade of Womens Land Army in Westgate Street, Gloucester, 28th September 1941

The Outdoor Life for Me . . .

The outdoor life did wonders for our complexions but was hell on the hands – the horses were indifferent.

(Photos: WLA Archives)

The Women's Timber Corps

The Women's Timber Corps followed in the footsteps of the Women's Forestry Corps in the 1914–18 war. The WTC, as a separate organisation, with its distinctive badge and green beret (and how pleased we were with our replacement for the WLA felt hat) did not come into being until 1942. Before that, forestry workers were enrolled as members of the Women's Land Army.

It was another organisation in which women were regarded with suspicion. Timber production was supposedly much too heavy work for women and they could not be expected to make an efficient and worthwhile contribution. Yet again, women proved that this initial assessment was totally unwarranted.

When the prospect of direction of labour loomed early in 1940, I decided to make my own choice before I was directed into something I should dislike. An article in one of the weekly illustrated magazines (*Picture Post*, I believe) about Land Girls doing forestry work persuaded me that this was the life for me, and I never regretted my choice. On my next half day I went to the WLA recruiting office in Gloucester and to the amazement of my family, I returned with half my uniform in a carrier bag. (Come to that, I thought I was only going to make preliminary enquiries.)

I was lined-up for training as a Timber Measurer and, in April 1940, I reported for training at the Forestry School in the Forest of Dean. For a while, on arrival, my fate hung in the balance, as at the time 21 was the age limit for measurers and I was only just 19. However, timber measurers were urgently needed and a 19–year-old one was better than none, so I was in. I was the only country girl on the course but even I found starting work at 7 a.m. and spending the morning on totally unfamiliar work out of doors was not conducive to concentrating on two two-hour lectures during the afternoon.

The majority of forestry workers lived in camps, working in groups in plantations or sawmills, carrying out all but the heaviest work of felling and converting timber. Before the war there were very few women employed in forestry work, probably no more than 200 or 300, and these only on the

Above – Bette Anderson (left) and Betty Bowes, Forest of Dean, 1940.

Top left – Timber Measurers' Training Course at Parkend Forestry School, April 1940. Bette Anderson, far left.

Bottom left – Timber measuring – Betty Bowes on left.

East Beat, Forest of Dean. WTC timber measurers. Bette Anderson second from left, standing, and Betty Bowes second from left in front, with civilian forestry workers.

lightest work. By the time the Women's Timber Corps started its independent life in 1942, there were over 1,000 "Lumber Jills" and by 1943 there were nearly 4,000 in England and Wales, with a further 1,000 in Scotland. Recruits were coming in at the rate of 200 or more a month, and at about this time further recruitment was ended. There were always as many volunteers as were needed and it was never necessary to direct anyone into the Timber Corps.

"Lumber Jills" were almost entirely engaged on production line work, under the Ministry of Supply Home Timber Production Department (later the Board of Trade) and very few worked with the Forestry Commission. In fact, the WTC was regarded with some degree of disfavour, as clear-felling comparatively young plantations for pit props, Army pickets, railway sleepers, etc. was

"slaughter trade" – felling trees long before they had reached maturity.

I was lucky in having had the opportunity to work in a number of different capacities as a "Lumber Jill" – as a timber measurer I coped with measuring up piece work, working out wages, stock recording and despatching. In our spare time we were expected to pitch in with any work that was going.

Later I went on to requisitioning. This entailed travelling round Gloucestershire and Wiltshire measuring and valuing standing timber for purchase, with one forestry officer, supervising the work of two or three girls and negotiating the final contracts (or sometimes compulsory purchase orders if landowners proved unco-operative).

Without doubt my most unfavourite job was charcoal burning. Even the extra soap coupons and "dirt money" did little to compensate for the penetrating, choking dust when one "broke" the kiln and bagged up the still warm charcoal, which was needed in large quantities for gas-mask filters.

Another job was similar to requisitioning. "Polecats" had a roving commission selecting suitable trees for telegraph poles and special purpose poles for the armed forces. Most of these had been imported pre-war and home-grown trees did not offer so many poles of equal quality to the imports.

A lift home at the end of the day – Forest of Dean.

In 1940 the *Quarterly Journal of Forestry* was asking for more forestry workers. 'The prejudice against employing women is surely a superficial one,' and the *Scottish Forestry Journal* was making the same appeal a year later.

In the same journal in 1942, James Tait wrote of an encounter with a 'squad of women without even the supervision of a man'. This squad consisted of a forewoman and six workers, thinning a stand of mixed hardwoods and conifers about 30 years old. Mr Tait continued, 'From what I saw of the work done and how these girls set about their duties, I am afraid I have to admit that mere man will have to take care if he is to be recognised as a forester in future. The woman in charge could lay a tree with the best of men, and it is some considerable time since I saw anyone so knacky in the handling of an axe . . . It would appear that the girls work in pairs and that they change their duties each day, and the two who are snedding one day may be felling the next and so on.'

In *Forest Service*, G. Ryle describes the exploitation of 'a large rough wood, amounting to a couple of hundred acres of heavy coppice grown oak, entirely with female labour and female administration. So successful was it that a sawmill for the manufacture of colliery tramline sleepers was quickly added for their working.'

There were some injuries from this heavy work with unfamiliar tools, but on the whole women came to terms with it very quickly. They learned to handle the razor-sharp tools efficiently and treat them with respect.

At times there were additional hazards. Eileen Rawlinson said, 'We suffered little injury but had a frightening experience when we were strafed by German planes around the edge of the clearing at the time of the heavy air raids over Ashford, Kent. These planes visited us on three separate occasions yet, apart from a peppered mess-hut, we were unharmed, having bolted for our lives into the cover of the trees.' She said, 'Air raids over Croydon were heavy and we had to be on the alert for incendiaries and bombs among the bracken'. A third move to Heathfield, Sussex also had its moments. 'We were in what was then known as "bomb alley" . . . most of our time was spent falling flat.' They were in an area where the RAF intercepted V2 rockets before they could reach London. Fortunately, very few "Lumber Jills" had such a hair-raising time.

In addition to the members of the WTC, a large number of women were employed locally, mainly in extensively wooded areas such as the Forest of Dean. Pre-war, there had been virtually no female labour, so there were no recognised piece-work rates. "Equal pay for equal work" was then an unheard of concept. The forester where I was working in the Forest of Dean asked me to do a spell on all the jobs which women might be expected to do, so

Above: Fye and Florence on felled timber at Rushyford.

Top left: Fye on a tractor.

Left: Fye and a colleague, Florence, sawing timber with a bow saw.

Timber Measurers

Fye Savage was in the first group of timber measurers to be trained. She says that at first her duties were measuring timber and working out the cubic content but 'daily our duties grew till we were handling wages, peeling and counting pit props, despatching props by road or rail, driving tractors, etc.' There were many hazards. Fye remembers how one problem was attending to the needs of nature in a male-dominated community.

Ngaire Dormand and Gladys Bainbridge.

A Tricky Job . . .

Ngaire Dorman and Gladys Bainbridge trained at Bury St Edmunds, and worked around Warwickshire, near Rugby, Leamington Spa, and Coventry. By the end of the first year they were swing 7 pound axes proficiently. For some time they were billeted in a large hostel for munitions workers in Coventry, where they were able to enjoy dancing and ENSA entertainments every night! They cleared brushwood, etc., after the men had felled large elms oaks, etc. Unfortunately, Gladys broke her elbow and was unable to continue with timber work. Shortly after Ngaire was transferred to Nottingham, near her home, cutting firewood and checking cordwood — a tricky job, she says — 'I had to watch the men didn't cheat by putting bent and twisted logs in the middle to make up the stacks'.

Left — Janet Duncan, Betty Patterson and Elsie Fowler at work in Beal, Northumberland

Right — Taking a break . . . (left to right) Monica Kirk, Dorothy Taylor, Ruth Mcfarlane (née Wilkinson), Mary Wilkinson.

Mary Wilkinson joined the WTC in 1940, and worked on Muncaster Castle estate in Eskdale, Carlisle and Ravenglas. She crosscut and stacked pit props, cut telegraph poles, and worked a portable saw bench. For a time she was at Green Garth Hostel, at Holmbrook in Eskdale.

Left – Beal 1944 –
Joan Waters, Ethel Slack
Grace Anderson, Janet Duncan, Irene Laws,
Joyce Marshall, Elsie Fowler, Maud Wilkinson.

Right – Beal again –
(from left to right)
top: Grace Anderson, Irene Laws, Joyce Marshall,
Janet Joan Waters,
bottom: Kitty Modlinski, Joyce Slack, Lily Modlinski,
Ethel Slack.

Left – Park End Forestry School
Timber Measurers Course April/May 1940

Right –Forestry Corps, RE.
The Author is on the far right.

By this personal message I wish to express to you

BESSIE DOREEN ANDERSON, W.L.A. NO: 29589

my appreciation of your loyal and devoted service
as a member of the Women's Land Army from

17.4.40   to   31.3.46

Your unsparing efforts at a time when the victory
of our cause depended on the utmost use of the
resources of our land have earned for you the
country's gratitude.

Elizabeth R

The personal message from HM Queen Elizabeth.

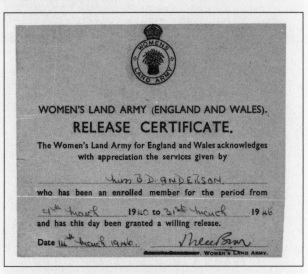

We were disappointed that our release documents made no mention of the Women's Timber Corps!

But the Ministry of Labour and National Service got it right and gave the occupation as WTC Measurer!

WTC Lewdown Camp, Devon, 1945.

that he could see how much an average woman would be able to do, from which he could work out appropriate piece-work rates. There was a different rate for each year up to 18. I can't remember the rates, but the minimum hourly rate for a school-leaver was about 3d. (a little over 1p).

It was hard work, often dirty, sometimes in cold, wet conditions, and not well paid (as with the Land Army, the Timber Corps got no post-war training or gratuity) but for me the opportunity to work in beautiful woodland surroundings was compensation for the hardships and I think this was so for most of the WTC.

Bette Anderson outside office on Stourhead Estate.

When the Forestry Section of the Women's Land Army became the Women's Timber Corps, our green beret replaced the WLA felt hat — we thought it a great improvement!

Entertainments

The value of entertainment as a morale booster was appreciated in the 1914–18 war and, in the light of his experience then, when war threatened in 1938 Basil Dean began making plans to organise shows for the armed forces wherever they might go. He also had in mind the civilians in armament factories, and his thoughts encompassed theatre, concert parties and music from symphony orchestras to jazz. So the Entertainment National Service Association was born, and by the end of the war *The Times* reported that ENSA had put on 2½ million performances for over 500 million members of the forces and munition workers. Four out of every five members of the profession worked for ENSA at some time.

"Every Night Something Awful" was coined by Tommy Trinder, and it must be admitted that the standards were variable, but that was an outcome of the enthusiasm of the entertainers and the overwhelming demand for shows. And a serviceman's wife may have written in a letter to a newspaper in 1943, 'I am disturbed to learn that ENSA is now at Malta. Don't you think the people on that island have been through enough?' But the men in the desert and the jungle gave a terrific welcome to the girls who toured and who danced and sang under incredibly difficult conditions. They put on carefree happy shows in tents and huts, on open stages or on the backs of lorries, often in freezing conditions in Europe and overwhelming heat in North Africa and the Far East.

The first ENSA concert took place on 10th September at Camberley, with Frances Day in the cast. At first there was some resistance to sending women to France with BEF, but Gracie Fields insisted that she should go and others quickly followed.

Six weeks after D-Day, six mobile theatres and sleeping caravans followed the invasion forces into France, and Jessie Matthews, Diana Wynyard and Margaret Rutherford were appearing in plays within hearing of the German artillery.

In the Far East, Edith Evans and the Waters sisters were among the first to tour, and only 10 miles from the fighting had to take cover in slit trenches in an air raid.

The tours by top line stars are well known, but not so much has been written about the girls who went on slogging round the circuits for months or years on end — girls like Doreen Scott, who *en route* for North Africa with the "Let's Have a Party" company, was in a Dutch vessel which was bombed by a German aircraft — they all got safely into lifeboats and 'the troops still on board sang songs to keep our spirits up'. After drifting for some hours they were picked up by an American ship and landed in North Africa. In spite of this misadventure, only one show of their planned programme had to be abandoned. Doreen Scott also toured in the Far East and worked with ENSA through most of the war years.

Parties in UK also toured munitions factories, giving concerts in canteens both for day and night shifts and some ENSA personnel visited air raid shelters during the Blitz.

In 1940 the "Council for the Encouragement of Music and the Arts" was started by the Pilgrim Trust, on a "classical" level. There was much more response to the music provided by CEMA than had been expected in some circles and it was soon government funded (in spite of Ernest Bevin's protests that it was 'too 'ighbrow').

Factory Concert Poster.

Patricia Braybon went straight from RADA to the permanent company at Salisbury Playhouse (then the Garrison Theatre). She stayed there until the end of hostilities in Europe, then went to India with an all-woman company of 17 in "Nine Till Six". She is portrayed as Patricia Froud in Wilf Thwaites' caricatures of the cast of "School For Heroes and "Yes and No".

(Cartoons by Wilf Thwaites)

startled at the first camp they visited to find that an enterprising entertainment officer had put up posters describing them as: 'Miss Constance Lambert and Miss Margot Fonteyn supported by a ballet of 40 lovely girls.'

In London Myra Hess began a series of lunchtime piano recitals in the National Gallery, and these proved so popular that she continued, running up an amazing total.

It was not only the professionals who provided entertainments – in many areas amateur dramatic societies, choirs, orchestras and concert parties were formed and toured local camps and factories.

In the *Warminster Journal* of 22nd March 1940 there was a paragraph: 'The formation of a concert party to tour the military camps and depots in and around Warminster is the object of a well-known stage artiste and dance instructress, Miss Renee Terry, who has lately come to reside in Warminster. Miss Terry is looking for amateur and semi-professional artistes who are prepared to entertain troops on payments of expenses only.'

Gracie Fields was one of the most popular of the many well-known stars who toured the theatres of war. In the first concert arranged by ENSA in France, she was the outstanding star turn in spite of ill-health and against her doctor's orders she insisted on appearing. She sang at two shows a day.

CEMA also aimed to make ballet and opera available to more people, and I, for one, have the happiest memories of seeing the Anglo-Polish ballet in Cheltenham and Bristol, and the Ballet Rambert at the Garrison Theatre in Salisbury. Members of the Land Army and Timber Corps were not admitted to all service amenities (I was actually turned out of quite a variety of service canteens, etc.), but I was so determined to see the Ballet Rambert that I went to the box office and very determinedly said, 'I intend to see this show. Can I buy a ticket for myself or must I go out and pick up a soldier to bring me in?' Luckily for me the officer in charge of the theatre happened to be in the box office and hastily said, 'Never let it be said that I forced a girl onto the streets – by all means come whenever you want to!'– I did!

Sadlers Wells Ballet also toured, accompanied by two pianos, with Constant Lambert conducting and playing one piano. Pre-war, ballet was regarded as rather an elitist form of entertainment and there were some doubts about their "box office appeal" – they were, however, somewhat

There was no soft living for the ENSA touring companies overseas. They often appeared in open-air "theatres" on hastily knocked up stages or on lorries. Photograph courtesy: Imperial War Museum.

Vera Lynn. *(Photo: Imperial War Museum)*

Below — Elsie and Doris Waters were among the first entertainers to go to India. Peter Watts, of the Chindit Road show said, 'The ones the Chindits really fell for were Elsie and Doris. The chaps described them as real ladies and they really were. They had style and they came over marvellously. There they were, in paddy fields and in the jungle, immaculately dressed and beautifully turned out. They went everywhere. They were super and absolutely charming.'

Sing with ENSA Poster.

(Photo: Imperial War Museum)

The same efforts were being made all over the country. Some of these well-meaning and enthusiastic groups were — shall we say — less than first-rate entertainment, but others were of very high quality and were warmly welcomed wherever they went.

One such was the "Non-Stop Variety Troop Show" based in Bournemouth, which had a remarkable record. Run by Betty Hockey in the Southern Command area, they ran four different shows and the full company consisted of 16. In spite of all working full time, they did three or four shows a week and by 1946 had done a total of 1,000 shows, and one of Betty's treasured possessions is a "Thank You" certificate from the Commanding Officer of Southern Command. Among Betty's happiest memories are of their visits to military hospitals, and of putting on shows at very short notice for returning prisoners of war at Southampton. 'These boys from Japanese camps', says Betty, 'were in a dreadful state, and the Non-Stops were privileged to be among the first white women the POWs had seen for a long time — how could the party refuse when requested to visit sometimes five nights in a row?'

Betty Hockey and her dancers and singers, and all the girls who worked for ENSA, CEMA and any other entertainment organisations undoubtedly made a very worthwhile contribution to the war effort.

Doreen Scott in ENSA uniform.

Doreen *en route* to North Africa was in a ship sunk by a torpedo. She and her companions spent some hours in a lifeboat before being picked up by an American ship. Nevertheless, only one show of Doreen's ENSA tour was cancelled.

Below — Doreen Scott and friends at the Pyramids after being rescued.

ENSA in Transit

Above – Doreen Scott with the troop in Burma.

Left – Troop in Tel Aviv, November 1944.

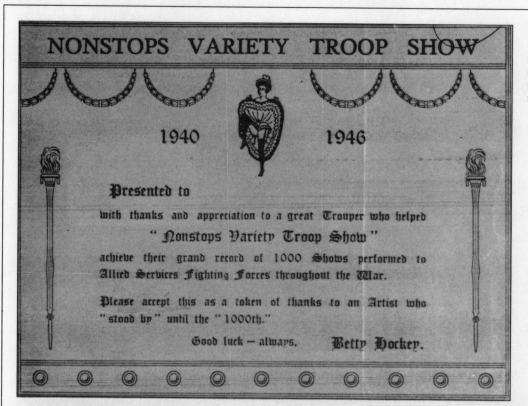

NONSTOPS VARIETY TROOP SHOW

1940   1946

Presented to

with thanks and appreciation to a great Trouper who helped

"Nonstops Variety Troop Show"

achieve their grand record of 1000 Shows performed to
Allied Services Fighting Forces throughout the War.

Please accept this as a token of thanks to an Artist who
"stood by" until the "1000th."

Good luck — always.   Betty Hockey.

Betty's thanks to the members of her party for their remarkable record of service.

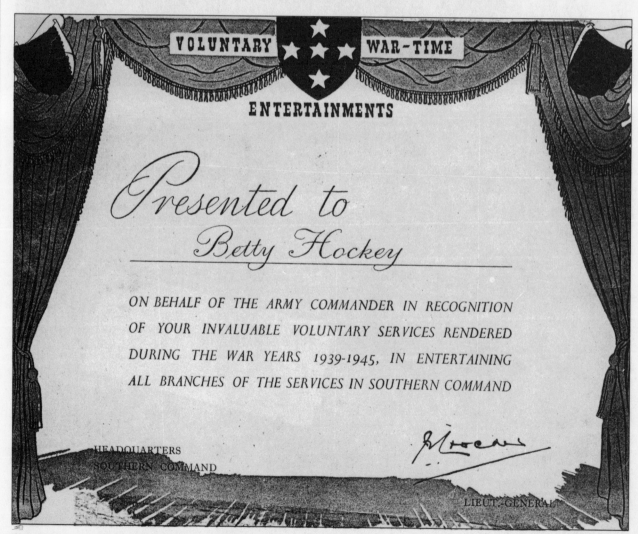

VOLUNTARY ★ WAR-TIME
ENTERTAINMENTS

Presented to

Betty Hockey

ON BEHALF OF THE ARMY COMMANDER IN RECOGNITION
OF YOUR INVALUABLE VOLUNTARY SERVICES RENDERED
DURING THE WAR YEARS 1939-1945, IN ENTERTAINING
ALL BRANCHES OF THE SERVICES IN SOUTHERN COMMAND

HEADQUARTERS
SOUTHERN COMMAND

LIEUT.-GENERAL

Betty Hockey's treasurer certificate of thanks from Southern Command for over 1,000 shows put on by her amateur group, the Nonstops.

Nonstops Concert Party poster.

Betty Hockey, Can-Can dancer.

Nonstops Variety Troop

All the members of the Nonstops concert party, run by Betty Hockey were unpaid volunteers and most of them were in full-time jobs. They went all over Southern Command, and before D-Day were putting on shows every evening for the troops who were restricted to their camp areas in the tense build-up to the invasion.

Members of the Nonstops on board a battleship in Bournemouth Bay.

Dame Myra Hess started piano recitals in the National Gallery shortly after the Second World War started. The lunchtime concerts proved tremendously popular and Dame Myra gave nearly 1,700 recitals. *(Photo: Imperial War Museum)*

Not all of ENSA's transport was as swish as this streamlined van, a gift from Gertrude Lawrence. *(Sunday Times Magazine)*

Ballet Goes to War — *Recollections from Christelle Cleaver*

Founded in 1935, Lydia Kyasht's Ballet de la Jeunesse Anglaise toured England and visited Denmark. In 1940 it adopted a less cumbersome name and, as Lydia Kyasht's Russian Ballet, presented an original and entertaining repetiore with Bebe de Rolande and Neville Astor as leading dancers. Lydia Kyasht Junior, Madame's daughter, created two ballets, *Heraldic* and *Ballerina*. Catherine Marks gave the company *Marie Antoinette*, *Cinderella* and *Derby Day*, a delightful comedy ballet based on Firth's famous painting. John Regan added a typical Russian folk tale, *Katyusha*, and Madame Kyasht produced *Chopiniana*, *Casse Noisette act II* and Anna Pavola's *Gavotte*.

War was declared and the Kyasht Company went into action under the auspices of ENSA – Entertainments National Service Association – which was where I came into the picture. One of Madame's girls had to have her appendix removed and I was nominated her replacement. This was in 1943, and although I am unable to corroborate the exact date, if my memory serves me correctly, I made my debut with the company dancing in Caterham Barracks in August/September. It was a cold debut.

We collected a wide range of insigna used by the British and Allied Armies to identify personnel and vehicles belong to the various divisions when we were dancing for them in the UK, and later in occupied Germany. We girls considered it a mark of true affection when one of our admirers gave us his shoulder flash. We sewed them onto webbing belts, which we called 'scalp' belts. I still have mine, complete with Guards division flash, Polar Bear flash and so on.

Above — The full company in *Casse Noisette act II* — Roy Gentry, Joan Grant, Joan Baynard, Joanna Denise, Gabrielle D'Arcy, Patricia Grant, Pamela Btesh, Pita Abbot, Ernest Marini, Joy King, Anita Walsh and June Lloyd.

Left — 'Madame' — Lydia Kyasht: 25-3-1882 – 11-1-1959, the first Russian Ballerina to dance in London.

Left to right – Letty, Patricia Grant, Joy King and Christelle Cleaver as villager run to inspect the girl 'puppet', Joan Banyard.

Katyusha

Katyusha choreographed by John Regan to a hotchpotch of melodies by Glazunov, Tchaikowski and Mussorgsky, and traditional folk tunes, was the only ballet the troops did not laugh of the stage, probably because it told a 'who-dunnit' tale and the fact that there were no men in white tights on its cast list.

Left – Katyusha, performed by Joan Grant, flings out her arms in a gesture of despair because her two children have wandered into the woods and not returned. They fall into the hands of a wicked puppeteer, who puts them into a deep hypnosis, dresses them in puppets's clothes and makes them dance for the villagers.

Christelle Cleaver in ENSA uniform. She wore a South African flash on her shoulder because she was travelling on a South African passport. She was at St Cyprian's School in 1939, and somebody on the staff applied for a passport for her — and it was not until 1944, when she was about to be posted overseas by ENSA that she realised that she had been incorrectly nationlised. Cape Town had issued her with a green South African passport, instead of a blue British passport. The error was later rectified.

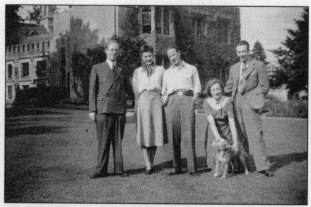

George Brown, our blind drummer. Unfit for the forces, signed on with ENSA and toured with the company.

George, Gabrielle, Ernest, Betty and Roy.

The house in the backgroud, then requisitioned and doing duty as an ENSA Hostel, is the beautiful manor house at Combe, Oxfordshire. The middle section between the two Tudor wings dates back to mediaeval times, and an underground passage links it to the church on the right.

Alma Edwards, Joan Grant, June Lloyd, Pita Abbot, Madame Kayasht, Anita Walsh, Letty Pamela Btesh and Joan Banyard.

Gabrielle D'Arcy, Joy King, Letty, Roy Gentry, Joan Grant and Patricia Grant.

Roy Gentry supports Betty Jones, our pianiste, Ernest Marini supports Gabrielle D'Arcy. George Brown supports Patsy, the Companys' cannine mascot.

Council of Voluntary War Workers

From the outset, much thought was given to the welfare of the armed forces, both at home and overseas and, at the instigation of the Army Council, the churches and christian organisations formed the Council of Voluntary War Workers to co-ordinate and assist in activities in connection with welfare and amenities for HM Forces.

The Council was made up of:

Young Men's Christian Association, Young Women's Christian Association, Catholic Women's League, Salvation Army, Church Army, Church of Scotland, Methodist and United Baptist Churches, Toc H, Army Scripture Readers, Soldiers' and Airmen's Christian Association, Church of England Soldiers', Sailors' and Airmen's Institute

The YMCA played a leading role and ran about half of the facilities provided.

Wherever the forces went, canteens, mobile and static, soon followed — first with "mobiles" and, as soon as practicable, with centres with comfortable lounges, libraries and entertainments.

In 1944 there were some 400 women in the Middle East. About two-thirds of the staff of over 200 centres and numerous mobile canteens were women, and up to 200 a month were being sent into NW Europe following the invasion forces. They were also represented in Iceland and India. In Athens a woman attached to Toc H kept a canteen going through the heaviest of the fighting.

In UK most of the larger railway stations had canteens on or near them, and hostels near major stations provided accommodation for a few hours' sleep, washing facilities and meals at odd hours for personnel in transit.

There were also YMCA mobile canteens to be found in London during the Blitz, dispensing hot drinks and snacks to rescue workers, firefighters, etc.

Canteens in many places acted as go-betweens for householders willing to offer a few hours of home comforts to serving men and women. Bath YMCA gave "Hospitality Cards" to service personnel, offering an introduction to a family, and many lasting friendships were formed — many mothers of serving men were happy to offer the hospitality they hoped their sons might be finding elsewhere.

Don Tuddenham, of Oldfield Park, Bath, remembers that going home was like 'going to

These men, all of them badly wounded, many of them limbless, are waiting for a ship to take them home to England. They are seen here at a tea-party at the YWCA, Tripoli, given in their honour by the Red Cross. Sergeant T. Rogers of Rotherham, Yorkshire, accepts another cake, while beside him Sergeant G. Kidd of Exmouth, Devon, smiles appreciatively at Carol Downs of the "Hello Happiness" ENSA party.

Right — YMCA "Stonk Club", Dortmund.

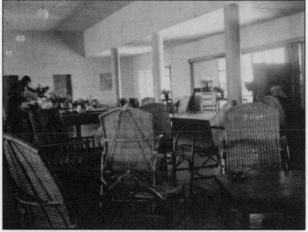

With the YWCA in the Middle East — The Suez Forces Club.

Left — Phyllis Ticehurst and Fay Williams in summer uniform.

and

Right — In winter uniform.

Below — Conference of workers from all over the Middle East. 'With our wonderful chief, Miss Jean Begg from New Zealand', Ismailia, June 1943.

Top left – Phyllis Ticehurst and Fay Williams, YWCA in Suez 1941/42

Top right – Phyllis Ticehurst, YWCA, Suez 1941.

Left – Phyllis Ticehurst with 'Sally, Blondie and Tiger', Suez November 1944.

Below – With colleagues at a Conference, Ismailia 1943.

A "mobile" damaged beyond repair in the Blitz was shipped to America on a fund-raising mission.

When the forces were firmly established in any theatre of war, book shops were set up.

another barracks', as his mother kept open house. She kept a record of her visitors – two exercise books, listing names, dates and meals – from 1940 to 1945 (her son estimates some 400 in all) – and left a box of affectionate and grateful letters from her boys and girls, and their mothers as well, and an album of photographs. There are cards from German and Italian prisoner of war camps, Christmas cards from all theatres of war and – sadly – one of her own letters "Return to Sender" and a letter from a mother telling of the death of her son. All telling a story of the great value of the warm hospitality offered by an ordinary housewife in an unpretentious suburban house, always ready to welcome visitors, in spite of the problems of rationing and acute shortages. She kept in touch with some of "her boys" until her death. Mrs Tuddenham was an outstanding example of warm-hearted generosity and motherliness, but a similar pattern was repeated all over the country.

At the peak there were over 4,000 hostels, clubs and canteens, and over 1,500 mobile canteens and over 75 per cent of the staff was female, over 50,000 women giving voluntary service – with these and the private hospitality instigated through them, there can hardly have been a man or woman in the armed services who was not grateful for their presence.

The Americans sent canteens to serve our forces.

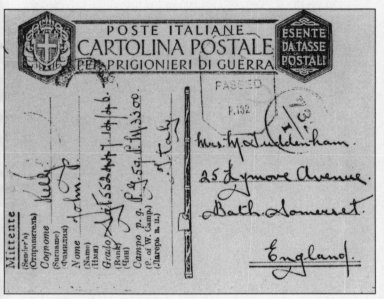

throughout 1940's . . .

from Algiers . . . from Germany . . . from Italy . . .

from wherever they were . . .

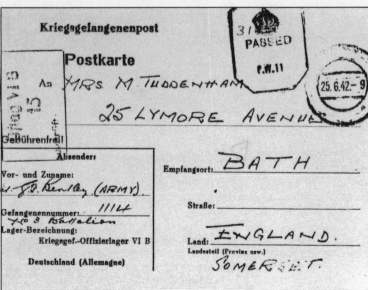

John Kelly, who sent the card from the Italian POW camp, is on the right in front of the photograph.

A page from Mrs Tuddenham's 'log' of visitors

Mrs Tuddenham offered to entertain service personnel in her home through the YMCA Hospitality Scheme in Bath, and her involvement was phenomenal! After their first introduction her "boys" returned again and again for 24 hour and 48 hour leaves as well as for tea or dinner, and when they were posted away kept in touch from every theatre of war, and from POW camps. Mrs Tuddenham's records show that she provided well over 600 meals – an impressive total, even with some coupons from the YMCA to supplement the meagre food rations.

Women's Royal Naval Service

The Women's Royal Naval Service approached recruitment on a different plan from the other women's services. There was no rapid mass recruitment but a steady build up, with each Wren being selected for a specific job.

In 1938, in a Government booklet a paragraph appeared, 'Women's Service in the Royal Navy' saying that initially about 1,500 women would be wanted for a very limited range of jobs. No age limits or other qualifications were mentioned, and in response to this short paragraph 15,000 letters were received from enthusiastic would-be recruits.

Many of the first Wrens were recruited from the families of naval personnel at naval stations where WRNS units were being formed. These "immobile" Wrens continued to live at home.

Numbers were smaller than in ATS or WAAF, as there were fewer shore-based men who could be replaced by women, but even so, the Admiralty

Recruiting poster.

estimate of 1,500 women was soon left far behind. By 1942 there were 40,000 Wrens serving in some 80 trades in the Navy and Fleet Air Arm. Apart from clerical, domestic positions, administrative work and driving, they trained as signallers, ship's mechanics, radio mechanics, air mechanics, boats' crews and torpedo Wrens. Later in the war some WRNS officers were trained as Boarding Officers. By 1941 Wrens were being drafted overseas. The first, all wireless telegraphists, went to Singapore, from where they were safely withdrawn and continued their service in North Africa.

Sadly, the Wrens suffered the heaviest blow to any of the women's services when, in 1941, a draft composed of 12 Cypher Officers, 10 WT Chief Wrens and a Naval Nursing Sister sailed for Gibraltar in a small merchant ship. The convoy was attacked by a pack of 12 submarines. The WRNS draft were all killed instantaneously by a direct torpedo hit. In spite of this devastating blow, volunteers immediately came forward, and a replacement draft was quickly sent out.

In port, Wrens served as despatch riders and with ambulances and armaments trucks. These were dangerous duties in the air raids which hit many ports, and all were carried out efficiently, with disregard for personal danger. Several Wrens were decorated for bravery in taking their launches to the aid of the crews of vessels which had been attacked.

A very small number of WRNS officers were commissioned with specialised qualifications, but the vast majority were drawn from the ranks. All cadets had to be recommended by a naval as well as a WRNS officer.

At the start of the war the WRNS was officially a civil establishment, which caused some administrative difficulties and anomalies. In 1941 it was decided to transfer the administration to naval channels — 'which was what it always should have been,' as Vera Laughton Mathews, Director of the WRNS throughout the war, says in *Blue Tapestry*.

There was a particularly strong feeling of family tradition in the WRNS, and many daughters of Naval and WRNS personnel followed in their parents' footsteps by volunteering for naval service. The Director herself received a telegram at the Admiralty which caused considerable amusement: 'Dreadfully sorry, Mummy darling. Confined to barracks this weekend.'

But the value of the Wrens' service is made very clear by an Admiralty general message sent out on

8th May 1945; to all stations at home and abroad:

From Admiralty.

IMPORTANT

The following message has been sent by the Board of Admiralty to the Director, Women's Royal Naval Service. At this historic moment the Board of Admiralty wish to record their high appreciation of the part played by the Women's Royal Naval Service in support of the Fleet and in the work of the Naval Commands throughout the war against Germany and her European Allies. The loyalty, zeal and efficiency with which the officers and ratings of the Women's Royal Naval Service have shared the burdens and upheld the traditions of the Naval Service through more than five and a half years of war have earned the gratitude of the Royal Navy.

The evacuation from Alexandria.

Travelling in dirty ammunition trucks.

On the LCT from Ismailia to the Princess Kathleen.

On the move

Dorothy Heigham was evacuated from Alexandria with the WRNS, when Rommel was advancing. The Wrens were allowed one suitcase – "civvies" and personal items seemed more important than uniform (a decision the Admiralty did not approve). Dorothy was on night duty on 30th June 1942 and after collecting pay went to bed at 11 a.m. only to be wakened at 12.00. She was told to pack and they left Alexandria by train. They travelled in cattle trucks with no provisions or toilets. They reached Ismailia at 5 a.m. where they were able to take a welcome wash and have a drink at the YMCA. After that they were bundled into dirty trucks and taken to the lake to board the Princess Kathleen. They sailed down the Suez Canal to Suez, where the ship waited to hear the outcome of the Battle of Alamein. Had it fallen they would have sailed on to South Africa. It was a difficult journey and wait at Suez. Each Wren had only one white uniform and had to take it in turn to stay in bed or wear swimsuits while it was washed. The Chinese crew went on strike and the Wrens had to clean the ship. On 6th July most of the refugees who had been aboard left, and air raids were not so bad. The girls were allowed ashore on alternate days, when they could go swimming and dancing with local troops. On 24th July they moved on again, to "The Aviary", a tented transit camp in the desert. It was surrounded by a wire fence. They arrived in a sandstorm and for the first night had to sleep on the sand, 10 to a tent, with only four showers between 200 girls. On 19th August they were sent to Cairo, where they lived in a wonderful palace with amazing painted ceilings and a harem (empty).

Mary Ferguson BEM

Mary Ferguson was awarded the BEM and Lloyd's Medal for Bravery at Sea for her courage when the *Avila Star* was torpedoed and sunk. She had been living in Argentina when war broke out, and decided to come to England to join the WRNS. She hoped that she would, after this experience, be able to become a woman sailor after the war.

Her voyage to England in 1942 proved to be a terrifying dramatic prelude to her naval service. When the *Avila Star*, an unescorted passenger liner, was some 300 mile from the Azores, she was torpedoed at night, all the lights went out, and while the lifeboats were being launched by trochlight, a second torpedo struck the ship, which sank rapidly, throwing many of the passengers into the sea.

Mary Ferguson says that she did not remember being catapulted into the water — 'I had a hit on the head, and woke up to find myself in the sea. There was a boat near so I clambered into it.' She was able to support two badly injured men, one of whom died later, and cared for them in a waterlogged boat throughtout the night. In the morning she was able to help them into another boat.

A friend of Mary's was in another boat, and when she saw her, Mary dived into the water and swam to join her — an unfortunate decision, as the boats lost touch with one another, and while the boat in which she transferred the injured men was soon picked up, the one to which she swam was 20 days at sea, before being found by a Portuguese sloop, which took the passengers to Lisbon. Of the 39 passengers in the lifeboat, 11 had died during their long exposure, and another died soon after being picked up. The friend Mary had gone to join was badly injured.

The citation for the BEM said: 'She showed great courage. She sat in the stern of a waterlogged boat throughout the night, nursing four injured men. When the Second Officer's boat came up at daylight she calmly dived over the side and swam to it.

She was covered in fuel oil, but she made no fuss about that, and her general behaviour during the 20 days ordeal that followed was magnificent.'

This traumatic introduction to life at sea did not deter Mary — as soon as she had recovered from her ordeal she joined WRNS as Boats Crew, and crewed boats at Devonport. She said: 'the sailors we ferried about sometimes asked about my ribbons, but, in spite of their own experiences, found it easier to believe that I had been decorated for playing football or pouring out cups of tea!'

Mary Ferguson in WREN's uniform — note her medal ribbons.

The lifeboat when first sighted by the Portuguese sloop which rescued Mary.

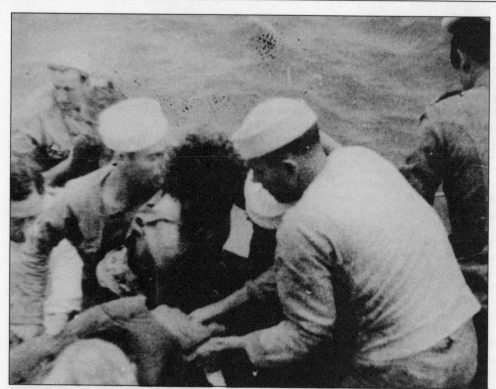

Mary being helped out of the lifeboat by Portuguese seamen.

WRENS recruiting poster.

Womens Royal Naval Service

O Almighty God, whose are the causes of righteousness on sea and land, the commander and defence of all that put their trust in thee: Bless thou and watch over these thy daughters in their stations of war, that they may serve with courage and constancy the Navies of our Sovereign Lord, King George, the security of his peoples, and thine own eternal purposes of good; through Jesus Christ our Lord

— Amen.

Almighty God, who art the protector of those who go down to the sea in ships, extend Thy blessing we beseech Thee, to the members of the Women's Royal Naval Service who go forth to the help of their brethen of the Royal Navy. Inspire them with the splendour of their cause: strengthen their resolution and confirm their loyalties, so that with dauntless hearts and dedicated wills they may work together for the coming of peace and the glory of Thy Kingdom upon earth, through Jesus Christ our Lord

— Amen.

Special prayers, written by a Wren Officer for the Westminister Abbey service on the fourth anniversary of the re-inauguration.

Auxiliary Territorial Service

There is no need in this book to extol the achievements of the ATS — their story continues today, and the value placed on them then is shown now by the fact that the range of their duties has continued to widen since the end of the war. The young women of today's WRAC will, I am sure, ensure that their forerunners, who laid the foundations of today's Corps are not forgotten.

In the early days "auxiliary" was the operative word, and their range of duties was narrow and unskilled. Women in the Army were "unsuitable" in the eyes of many people — again women were trying to usurp man's role.

After the formation of the WAAF in 1939 from the dual service, the ATS settled into its purely Army role, and at the outbreak of war already had a strength of nearly 20,000, and an immediate doubling of this number was decided on. At this time recruitment was on a regional basis, under the County Territorial Associations, and only five categories were open to women — drivers (only lighter vehicles), clerks, cooks, orderlies and storekeepers.

It was not until April 1941 that the ATS was given equal military status with the men, and came fully under the provisions of the Army Act, while ATS officers held the King's Commission, and, with the passing of the National Service Act in December 1941, women were liable to conscription. The first conscripts were called up in March 1942. There was, however, one difference from the men — women could not be required to work with lethal weapons without giving their written consent.

Living accommodation, unfortunately, could not keep pace with the rapid increase in numbers of recruits. Conditions were rough in many camps and were hampered by lack of necessary supplies. Also, there were lurid rumours — quite unfounded — of drunkenness and immorality. It was not until a report, commissioned by the Government, into living conditions, amenities and welfare of all three women's services, was published in the summer of 1942, which not only disproved the adverse stories, but showed that in actual fact illegitimate pregnancies in the services were fewer than in the civilian population of similar age, that the unpopularity of the women's services decreased, both with prospective recruits and worried parents.

Recruiting poster.

Princess Elizabeth.

I feel I cannot let you leave 21 Army Group on your return to civil life without a message of thanks and farewell. Together we have carried through one of the most successful campaigns in history, and it has been our good fortune to be members of this great team. God Bless you and God speed.

B. L. Montgomery

FIELD MARSHAL
COMMANDER IN CHIEF

BAOR·1945

Field Marshal Montgomery's farewell message to 21 AG.

General Headquarters, Home Forces.

Cpl. (A/Sgt) G.G.M.C.WEBB.

Auxiliary Territorial Service.

Your name has been brought to the notice of the Commander-in-Chief, Home Forces.

I am authorised by him to signify, by the award to you of this Certificate, his appreciation of the good service which you have rendered.

I have given instructions that a note of your devotion to duty shall be made on your Record of Service.

*Lieutenant General,
Chief of the General Staff,
to the Commander-in-Chief, Home Forces.*

Date 11th January, 1943.

Certificate in appreciation of good service to Cpl (A/Sgt) C. G. M. C. Webb.

The photograph above shows the Princess Royal inspecting the ATS at Bovington.

Miss W. Lamperd joined an ATS Territorial unit formed in Blandford Forum, Dorset, before the war. She was posted to Bovington Camp the day before war was declared and was immediately made up to a Sergeant.

3 Platoon, B Company at No & ATS Training Centre, Guildford, 16th November 1942.

Sue Crook on a predictor.

Sue Crook (née Woolston) of Woking, was a member of a mixed anti-aircraft battery. She was No. 1 in a predictor team (standing second from right in the photograph above).

The ATS at No. 1 Sub-depot, 1944.

Take Post

In a booklet *Take Post* which was issued to each member joining a battery it was stressed that 'The efficiency and effectiveness of the guns depend on the efficiency of the predictor. The efficiency of the predictor depends only on the efficiency of its operators. Do you realise that the protection of some vital area, of many of our people, is literally in your hands?' In March 1944 Sue's battery boarded a troop train to an unknown destination. At 0200 hours they arrived at Hove and had to march 1½ miles to a command post where they checked instruments, ate breakfast and did a full day's work. From then on life became hectic. Day and night they were rushing to the Command Post, 'having thrown battledress over pyjamas, with boots on but unlaced, and legs like jelly as we ran, our steel helmets weighing heavily on half-awake heads'. This was the build-up to D-Day. Later the battery moved on to Eastbourne and lived under canvas in Prince's Park, dealing with "Doodle-bugs". At one time actions were so frequent that the girls had to try and catch sleep in chairs adjacent to the post.

Ilfra Crow joined the ATS in the spring of 1939, and was called up on 3rd September. In December 1943 she was posted to East Africa. The convoy went through the Mediterranean and was attacked twice. Some ships were lost. They sailed through the Suez Canal and disembarked at Mombasa, from where they took a long train journey to Nairobi. Ilfra says, 'It was a very different life to the years since 1939. The tension was not there. We were working in various departments of a clerical company, some in the centre of Nairobi, and others out in the country. There was much to be done, covering Uganda, Kenya and Tanganyika. I assure you it was a very busy command and had connections with the East. The comradeship was marvellous and leaves up country were very popular. Later, when the time came to clean up all the command as it had been, East Africa had become so much our home it was very sad to leave.'

Ilfra Crow and a friend in the garden of Kewalu Hotel, Musaka, Uganda.

In 1941 this ATS poster caused a considerable stir — it was discussed in the House of Commons, and within a week it was withdrawn as being much too glamourous!

By the end of the war women were working in over 100 capacities and were carrying out highly-skilled technical duties. They served on anti-aircraft batteries as instrument operators, plotters and radio location operators; as kine-theodolite operators on gunnery practice ranges and as assistants on experimental gunnery units. In REME they trained as mechanics, working on tank repairs, as armourers repairing small arms and machine guns and as technicians testing compasses, telescopes and other apparatus.

Only volunteers were sent overseas, until 1945 when it was decided that single women might be drafted, but there were ATS volunteers with BEF in France in 1940. Telephonists in the Royal Corps of Signals stayed at their posts in Paris until 13th June and left only a few hours before the Germans surrounded the city. An attempt was made to set up another switchboard, but it had to be abandoned, and the ATS personnel landed in England on 16th June.

Early in 1941, the first contingents left for the Middle East, where they were able to release many men to fight in the desert. The ambulance units maintained a steady service, maintaining their own vehicles and carrying the wounded over rough roads, with cool disregard for minimal conveniences in their living conditions and danger from enemy air attacks.

Pat Hall was an ambulance driver with the ATS unit in Alexandria in 1942, and after the fall of

Postcards featuring the services were quite common in the First World War but were unusual in World War II. Above is a World War II card.

Poster — for War Service Grants for the Womens' Services.

Tobruk in June, when many personnel were being evacuated, she wrote in her diary on 2nd July, 'Gloom at our prospects turned to jubilation when the DDMS came in to assure us that we shall stay in Alex as long as the medical service stay. He was adamant that as drivers who knew the area and the ways of the hospitals we were irreplaceable,' and furthermore the Area Commander considered them 'good for morale'. And stay they did throughout what she calls "The Flap", giving invaluable service, and soon noted, 'It was extraordinary how quickly we all got used to having Rommel on our doorstep.' Some weeks later the Fleet returned to the port, and the Naval Chief of Staff (a friend of her family) asked Pat when she had got back — got back? Pat Hall delightedly wrote in *What a Way to Win a War*, 'It cannot often happen that a junior member of the most junior corps in the Army scores such a notable victory over the top brass of the Senior Service.'

Right—Audry Streeting (front centre) was very keen to join the ATS and as she was only 17 when she volunteered, it was suggested that she should join a local unit — a suggestion welcomed by her parents. The only vacancies were in the cookhouse, so she became a cook, she was later sent on catering courses, and served throughout the war as an NCO in the Catering Corps.

After Dame Helen Gwynne-Vaughn's retirement in 1941, the glamourous Jean Knox (left) was appointed Chief Controller of the ATS. She immediately gave the Service a new image by having the unflattering uniform restyled.

(Photo: Imperial War Museum)

'The Gentle Sex' travel by train.

(Photo: Imperial War Museum)

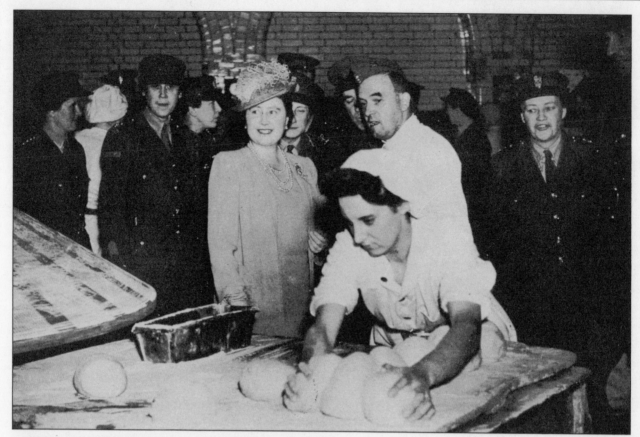

Her Majesty the Queen inspecting the Machine Bakery at Aldershot in 1944. The greatest test for the ATS girls who trained as bakers came in the same year when, during ten days before D-Day, the girls baked huge quantities of long-life bread for the invasion forces.

(Photo: Imperial War Museum)

Sub Officer Brown, S/Leader Morrison-Bell, 2/Sub Vortman, S/Leader Bolt, Sub Costeran, Controller Chitty and Controller Carlisle at a conference at the YMCA, Suez, 2nd October 1943.

(Photo: Imperial War Museum)

An ATS Vehicle Maintenance Team in action. The technical training courses for ATS mechanics were slightly longer than those for male soldiers, but the standards were exactly the same. *(Photo: Imperial War Museum)*

ATS offloading fuel for the tanks. *(Photo: Imperial War Museum)*

Women's Auxiliary Air Force

Although the Women's Royal Air Force started at the same time as the RAF in World War I, the Women's Auxiliary Air Force was not formed until 1939. Before that, personnel of the force had done duty for a year in RAF companies of the Auxiliary Territorial Service. The first was No. 2 RAF County of London ATS Co.

It was originally intended not to mobilise existing WAAF personnel until several months after the outbreak of war but in August 1939 an Air Ministry instruction mobilised them with immediate effect and authorised recruitment for specific trades.

The division between Army and Air Force in the ATS was at times totally arbitrary. In one case, described by Wing Officer Hope Melhuish, and quoted by Katherine Beaumont in *Partners In Blue*, a group at a training course was divided down the centre of the room. One side found themselves in the ATS and the other in the WAAF.

Joan Cupples stepped forward when drivers were asked for and was told that the WAAF needed drivers, and so her WAAF service commenced. In fact not all who had volunteered were employed as drivers.

In September 1939 the WAAF comprised 234 officers and 1,500 airwomen. The officers were appointed only for administrative duties, while the airwomen could only be employed in administration as clerks, become cooks or kitchen orderlies, equipment assistants, balloon fabric workers or drivers.

Numbers increased very rapidly and the range of duties widened steadily. By early 1940 numbers had risen to 360 officers and over 8,000 airwomen. By the end of that year they were substituting for men in 18 trades, and by the end of the war there were some 182,000 women in the WAAF – 16 per cent of overall RAF strength and 22 per cent of RAF strength in the United Kingdom.

WAAF Recruiting poster.

Recruiting maxims for RAF and WAAF.

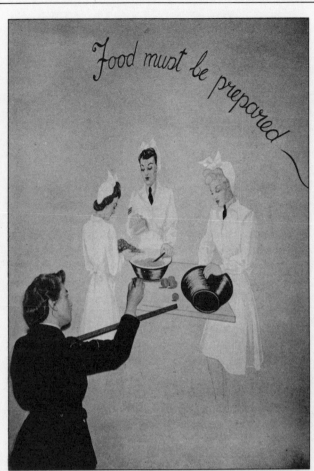

The Blue Room, the Recruiting Room at HQ, WAAF recruiting at Victory House, Kingsway, London, was redecorated in 1943 at the request of the CO who asked for something depicting both RAF and WAAF with some glamour. Murals were designed by ACW1 Richter, who painted them with the help of ACW1 Kingsley, ACW2 Kalker and LAC Robertson. The photographs on this page show the redecorating in progress. The revamped Blue Room opened on 1st April 1943 and remained so until two or three years after the war.

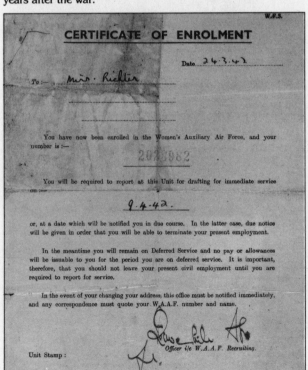

W.F.S.

CERTIFICATE OF ENROLMENT

Date 2 4 3 4 2

To :— Miss Richter

You have now been enrolled in the Women's Auxiliary Air Force, and your number is :—

2013982

You will be required to report at this Unit for drafting for immediate service on :—

9.4.42.

or, at a date which will be notified you in due course. In the latter case, due notice will be given in order that you will be able to terminate your present employment.

In the meantime you will remain on Deferred Service and no pay or allowances will be issuable to you for the period you are on deferred service. It is important, therefore, that you should not leave your present civil employment until you are required to report for service.

In the event of your changing your address; this office must be notified immediately, and any correspondence must quote your W.A.A.F. number and name.

Officer i/c W.A.A.F. Recruiting.

Unit Stamp :

(*9046) Wt. 45307—3130 20,000 2/42 T.S. 700

Left – Certificate of Enrolment – Miss Richter

Officers were serving in 15 categories and airwomen in 59 airman trades plus 21 trades special to the WAAF.

For the first two years the WAAF was in a strange relationship with the RAF. Although it was an integral part of the RAF organisation and administration, it functioned under a different code of discipline. WAAF officers were regarded by station commanders as merely advisory "specialists" in purely WAAF matters, with no executive authority in their own right, and restricted to those matters considered (by the senior male officers) to be exclusively "feminine".

It was not until the Defence (Women's Forces) Regulations were introduced in April 1941 that the status of the WAAF was resolved. It was declared that all members of the WAAF were members of the Armed Forces of the Crown, and the Air Council was empowered to apply the Air Force Act to the WAAF.

One of the trades opened to the WAAF at the instigation of the Air Ministry was that of Balloon Operator – despite the protests of the Commanding Officer of Balloon Command and his WAAF Staff Officer. In April 1941 20 balloon fabric workers volunteered and underwent a 10 week training course. They proved highly competent,

and substitution for men went ahead steadily, at first at the rate of two WAAF for one airman, but eventually at the rate of 14 to nine. By the end of 1942 15,700 WAAF had replaced 10,000 airmen, releasing them for other trades.

Women trained as mechanics, armourers and electricians. They played a full part in the testing and maintenance of planes, armaments and equipment.

One field in which WAAFs proved to have great aptitude was photographic interpretation, and they did valuable work at RAF Medmenham. Constance Babington Smith was one of the first WAAFs to be employed on this work and she made aircraft recognition her special study. It was thanks to her identification of V1 and V2 rockets on the ground, and from this their launch sites, that the RAF was able to bomb the launch sites and minimise the damage done by these weapons. Sarah Churchill and Dorothy Garrod worked extensively on aerial photographs of the North African coast, and provided information for "Torch" landings.

Three George Crosses and six Military Medals were awarded to WAAF personnel. A number of awards were made to WAAF officers who entered Europe with SOE.

One of a series of postcards. With the WAAF Balloon fabric workers.

Eugene asked for a girl in the WAAF who 'would not mind' having her hair styled. Sgt Shingles was pleased to oblige and her photograph was extensively used in newspaper adverts for Eugene Waving.

Skilled work on instrument repairing.

At work on aero engines: flight mechanics checking valve timing.

Armourers are here being taught how to mount guns on a Spitfire aircraft – work which calls for a fair amount of physical strength and a reasonably good education. Airwomen in this branch of the WAAF instal, inspect and maintain gunnery equipment of all kinds in aircraft: in addition, they deal with camera guns.

After repair and inspection, parachutes are hung up at full length to remove creases. Next they are packed in readiness for testing and are then repacked for issue.

Daily Rates of Pay of Airwomen of the Women's Auxiliary Air Force

Rank	Group I	Group II	Group III	Group IV	Group V	Group M
	s. d.	s. d.	s. d.	s. d.	s. d.	s. d.
A.C.W. 2nd Class ..	2 6	2 4	2 0	2 2	1 4	1 4
A.C.W. 1st Class ..	3 0	2 10	2 6	2 8	2 4	2 6
L.A.C.W.	3 8	3 4	2 10	3 0	2 8	2 10
Corporal	5 0	4 4	3 4	3 8	3 0	3 6
Sergeant	6 4	5 8	4 4	4 8	4 0	4 8
Flight Sergeant ..	7 8	6 8	5 4	5 8	5 2	6 4
Warrant Officer ..	9 4	8 4	7 8	7 8	7 8	9 0

A.C.W. = Aircraftwoman.   L.A.C.W. = Leading Aircraftwoman.   Group I (Radio and Wireless Mechanics) experimental at present.

Rates of pay, 1942 (1s. = 5p.; 1d. = [1/12] of 5p).

Above – Sergeant Elizabeth Mortimer (left) and Acting Section Officer Corporal Elspeth Henderson were two of the three Biggin Hill WAAF to be awarded the Military Medal.

(*Photo: RAF*)

The Menu RAF Medmenham, Christmas 1944. There are signature on the back of the Officers who waited on us including Group Captain Cator.

Below – The bride is Corporal McCall, and the bridesmaid, her sister, is also Corporal McCall, both from RAF Medmenham.

Above – Four very new recruits of three weeks, Morecombe Bay Training Depot, April 1942.

Air Transport Auxiliary

Between the wars there were great advances in aviation and the 1930s were the heyday of private owners' flying clubs. European aero clubs offered a round of social activities and there was a warm welcome everywhere for the increasing numbers of enthusiastic young pilots. There was little red tape to impede international flights.

The members looked for a way to turn their ability to good use and, as the possibility of war increased, the Civil Air Guard was formed. It aimed to train flying club members to be ready to fulfil a useful purpose should the need arise. What this purpose might be was not very clear. The CAG was subsidised and experienced pilots were trained as instructors. Some, such as Lady Rosemary du Cros, flew with Army co-operation, flying along the coast while anti-aircraft gunners practised training their guns on the plane.

When war came, many CAG members went into the RAF or the WAAF, but there was no prospect of flying in the WAAF, so some of the women pilots looked towards Air Transport Auxiliary. This was a civilian organisation formed to ferry planes from factories to operational airfields, and at first was on the strength of British Overseas Airways Corporation. The pilots were mainly men who were not acceptable to the RAF for reasons of age or low physical grades, and it was soon found that there were not enough pilots available for the volume of work.

Early in 1940, Pauline Gower was asked to form a small women's section. Initially eight women were invited to enrol. They were all experienced pilots with many flying hours to their credit, and they were tested by a BOAC instructor. It was not a popular innovation; it was said to be a man's job and women should not be used on it while many men were still unemployed. The fact that these men were not trained pilots and there was no time to train them was not taken into consideration.

At first the women pilots were stationed at Hatfield, Hertfordshire, where de Haviland Tiger Moths were manufactured. They were only allowed to fly these small trainer planes. It was a very difficult time for them, with adverse publicity and male prejudice to counter. An occasional accident by a male pilot would have been shrugged off but the female pilots knew that the smallest mishap in a plane flown by a woman would be greeted by a chorus of 'Obviously they can't cope with the job – we told you what would happen.'

However, the first eight women did all that was asked of them competently and showed by their efficiency that the adverse criticism was unwarranted. After a few months there was a steady intake of women. As the

No. 15 Ferry Pilots Pool ATA Hamble, 1943. Middle row: 4th from right, Rosemary du Cros; 5th, Margaret Gore, the CO next to her, Phillippa Booth. The only man was Jack Brown, flight engineer.

volume of work increased they were upgraded to other classes – Class II, single-engined fighters; Class III, simple two-engined planes; Class IV, twin-engined planes such as Wellingtons, Hudsons, Mitchells, etc; Class V, four-engined bombers (only 11 women qualified in Class V).

Initially, the young male fighter pilots, justifiably proud of their skills, did not take kindly to seeing their powerful machines confidently handled by girls. They felt that their image was diminished when it was seen that women could handle the planes, though obviously handling them in a fight was very different from straightforward, careful delivery flights.

In *ATA Girl*, Rosemary du Cros quotes an amusing story from a war book by 'an important Air Force officer'. His squadron was to be re-equipped with Mosquitoes, then the newest, fastest aircraft, and were very proud of being among the first to get these "wonder planes". When the first three Mosquitoes were brought in by the ATA everyone came out onto the tarmac to watch them land. The first Mosquito landed, taxied up to the control tower, and the pilot who climbed out was a pretty little blonde. The second came in, and the pilot was a man with one arm. When the third taxied up, out climbed the pilot – a small elderly woman clutching a knitting bag. Rosemary du Cros says that this may have been something of an exaggeration, though all three descriptions would have been applicable to ATA pilots at some time.

In 1941 it was decided to make Hamble an all-female depot and it stayed so until the end of the war. Later, Cosford also became an all-woman depot. By August 1941 there were 49 women pilots, and Lord Sempell said of them, 'Miss Gower and her girls have delivered something in the neighbourhood of 3,900 machines, and of these only one was a write-off and only 14 slightly "bent". There is no transport organisation of any kind with a better record than that.'

By 1944, there were 100 pilots (20 per cent of the total strength) handling 121 different types of aircraft, and they had delivered some 80,000 planes, including four-engined bombers. Apart from some of the heavy four-engined planes, which needed an additional flight engineer, all the deliveries were flown solo. On the all-female bases, the Anson "taxi" planes were also serviced by women and eventually, out of a total of some 2,000 ground staff, about 900 were women.

There were few sophisticated aids for flying to rely on. Weather forecasts were sketchy and there was no radio communication. Direction finding was by OS maps and sight of the ground. At the beginning of the war it was not permitted to mark either new airfields or barrage balloon sites on maps carried by the pilots. Most of the new airfields were to some extent camouflaged. Pilots had to study the master map before take-off, memorising as well as they could, roads, railways and any features marking the whereabouts of their destination airfield. There was a very occasional brush with enemy aircraft but probably the worst enemy was the weather. The greatest problem was drawing a safe balance between the urgency of the work and the uncertainty of weather conditions.

It was a gruelling life. Pilots reported for duty at nine, were allocated flights, possibly being taxied to another airfield to collect their machines. On delivery, if there was not another plane to take on, or a "taxi" at the aerodrome or one nearby, they had to make their own way back to base, either by train or possibly hitching a lift on another plane. They flew six days a week and had two weeks holiday a year. The working day could cover the hours of daylight. A specimen day from Lettice Curtis's log-book demonstrates the extent of the strain:

Taxied from White Waltham to Brooklands
Wellington HX598 – Brooklands to Little Rissington
Spitfire EP410 – Little Rissington to Llandow
Mosquito DD671 – St Athan to Ford
Mustang AG505 – Ford to Lichfield
Taxied by Puss Moth from Lichfield to Castle Bromwich
Wellington X9707 – Castle Bromwich to White Waltham

This was an unusual day – more usually it would be two or three flights at most.

There was neither time nor available machines for individual training on every type of plane. "Handling Notes" were prepared which were very comprehensive and covered every aspect of handling, but for day to day use a concise format was evolved. This covered all essential points – six inch by four inch cards, in ring binders, which would lie flat at the required page. 'A ferry pilot has so much to learn and remember that it is important he should not be taught one unnecessary fact.'

There were some casualties but they were few in view of the unavoidable risks. Fifteen per cent of pilots died – 129 men and 14 women. Amy Johnson was one of the casualties. She was flying in bad weather conditions, the wind had drifted her to the east and her petrol ran out while she was searching for her position. She was, in fact, over the Thames Estuary. She parachuted out but, in spite of naval vessels in the vicinity, she drowned.

The ATA uniform was navy blue with a fore-and-aft cap, gold wings and stripes. It featured Air Force blue shirt, black tie, black silk stockings and black shoes. Their badge was the initials ATA surrounded by oak leaves, and surmounted by an eagle.

In *ATA Girl*, Rosemary du Cros recounts many amusing incidents but there is no doubt about the strain of flying under these conditions. As the war dragged on and everyone got more and more tired she says, 'Any person capable of doing something did it. All those petty little barriers that are put up in peacetime to make society more pleasant melt away in a big crisis and life becomes a grim struggle of tired grey people all doing whatever it is they can do.'

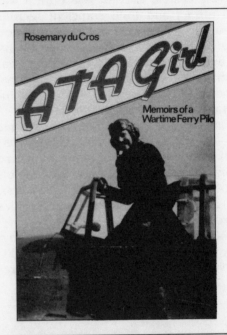

Lady du Cros (centre) and colleagues.

Lady du Cros flying her own Hawk Major.

135

Royal Observer Corps

In 1938 the Home Office was convinced that national coverage by an Observer Corps was essential for all aspects of civil defence. From that time expansion was rapid. The numbers required to cover the whole country was running into hundreds of thousands. Even at this time it was not easy to attract and train sufficient recruits. As more and more men were called up, and hours of work for civilians got longer, the problems increased but it was not until 1941, when it was clear that men of 35—40 not in reserved occupations could not expect further deferment, that the enrolment of women was authorised.

The first women enrolled went mainly into the centres – the observer posts in many places were in tough outdoor conditions. Before women could be incorporated into the close-knit bands of men (many of whom did not welcome the incursion of women) adequate toilet and washing facilities had to be provided.

In 1942 there was a major reorganisation of the ROC. By then the 4,000 full-time and 30,000 part-time included 650 women. A year later there were some 2,700 women.

In 1943 tests were inaugurated, practical and oral, on post and operation instructions and recognition of 50 aircraft. This test was compulsory but there were further, intermediate and advanced stages identifying 180 out of 200 different views.

Observers on the posts tracked all movements of enemy aircraft and RAF planes. They reported to ROC control rooms. Here the movements were plotted and the information passed on to RAF Fighter Command control centres. The Observer Corps was never a high-profile organisation. It is easy to under-estimate the value of their continuous and meticulous logging of air movements. Not only was their work of incalculable value to the air defence of the country, but they also gave assistance and guidance to lost or crippled aircraft returning from the Continent.

After the end of the war *The Aeroplane* summed up the achievements of the corps: 'The general public knew nothing of the activities of the ROC, and little realised that the one organisation which was in closest contact with operations of war was this pseudo-military body. In fact the ROC was probably responsible for more damage to the enemy's war effort than most of our home-based military forces of a similar character, which must be unique in the annals of civilian national service.'

Left – Joan Holifield joined the Observer Corps early in the war. when it was still a voluntary service. She worked in the Plotting Centre at Derby. There was a mapped plotting table, divided into squares. Around it were 12 listening positions connected to three posts, where aircraft spotters identified overhead planes and reported movements to the centre. From their phoned information tokens were placed on the table indicating type, numbers, height, direction, etc. As the planes travelled over the area, the information was passed on to adjacent posts and centres. On a raised platform, senior members of the corps, overlooking what was happening, passed the information on to the RAF and other services concerned. A mapped record was made of all movements. Many sessions were very quiet, even boring. 'P3 calling, I have an Anson (training plane) here.' 'Only an Anson' became a catch-phrase. But plotting bombers and fighters away on missions was more exciting. Unfortunately, it was sad to record fewer planes returning. One day, Joan remembers plotting a hedge-hopping Messerschmit and being instrumental in helping to destroy it. Members of the corps were able to visit observation posts to meet the spotters on the other end of the phones and see how they worked. Members were also able to visit an operational airfield. In quieter times there was aircraft recognition to learn from cards, though Joan says she doubts whether she would ever have been able to identify the real things without the help of the cards.

Navy, Army and Air Force Institutes

A comprehensive canteen service for all branches of the forces was regarded as of paramount importance, and in the inter-war years, the Navy, Army and Air Force Institutes had been set up. Plans were drawn up for the service which it was anticipated would be needed in the event of war. When the time came, these plans had considerably underestimated the needs and complexities of what would be required of NAAFI.

Pre-war, about 55 per cent of NAAFI staff were women, and by 1943 this percentage had risen to 85 per cent. At the peak over 60,000 women were employed. The canteens went wherever the troops went, and civilian employees overseas would have raised problems, so all personnel had to be under military control and discipline. In addition, it was desirable that if taken prisoner they should have the safeguard given to combatants under the Geneva Convention, so NAAFI girls went overseas as ATS/EFI (Expeditionary Forces Institutes), wearing ATS uniforms. They did their basic military training at ATS training depots and sub-sequently girls were enrolled in the ATS for EFI duties.

When an Army camp was set up a canteen followed. In the early months of the war these canteens were frequently ill-equipped in huts or tents. They were sometimes so inadequate that washing up had to be done outside. It was a desperate race to recruit and train staff to keep pace with the proliferation of camps and the girls frequently had to work exhaustingly long hours to keep their service going.

In North Africa, the first ATS/EFI girls went out in 1943, shortly after the victory of El Alamein. When they arrived at Suez they had a tremendous reception — troops lined the quayside as they disembarked. As they were often the only British girls in the command, they were overwhelmed with invitations for their off-duty hours. It was so overwhelming that a system was instituted whereby anyone wishing to escort "Miss Naffie" or "Miss Effie" had to sign a receipt and give an undertaking to return her to her quarters at a certain time.

NAAFI recruiting poster.

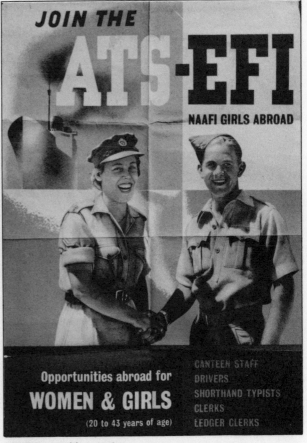

ATS/EFI recruiting poster.

NAAFI's ATS/EFI Depot – basic ATS training was undertaken by all personnel going overseas. (*Photo – NAFFI*)

The parade at the end of basic training was of military precision. (*Photo – NAFFI*)

The girls staffed many of the "road houses" along the route from Tobruk to Benghazi. They set up full-scale canteen services, in huts or tents, supplying meals, tea, coffee and beer. They also sold soap, toothpaste, toilet and personal items. Despite primitive and uncomfortable conditions they remained cheerful and their presence was as welcome as the goods they sold. An old 8th Army sergeant says, 'We'd have paid them for their smiles, if they hadn't had any beer. You can't know what it meant to come back out from the desert and see a lass from home up to her elbows in washing up!'

Early in 1944 an advance party of 16 were sent to Italy to set up the NAAFI service. By the end of the year there were over 100 there. At Rimini they earned the distinction of being the only ATS girls to serve with the 8th Army in the field.

Of their service in Italy, at the end of the war Captain John P. Shepherd, OC of 831 General Transport Company RASC, wrote, 'May I take this opportunity to place on record my appreciation and thanks to ATS/EFI drivers, CME, 60 of whom I had the honour to have attached to my Company, some of them at Bari and Rome, and most of them at Naples. These very fine English women came to us when we were hard-pressed for drivers, with the battle still on — their great spirit and team-work helped us at one of our peak periods. The records show that the tonnage carted by these drivers was always between two and three thousand tons per week, which meant hard going, sitting over red-hot engines during very hot weather, but never did any of them complain or grumble, and the next morning, on the early parade, they looked always fresh, clean and as smart as ever.'

It was not only adverse road and weather conditions that the girls had to contend with. Driver Evelyn Blanch Wood was attacked by armed bandits near Naples and her vehicle was stolen. It was not until she was forcibly thrown out that the bandits were able to drive the truck away.

When the build-up in the south of England began prior to the D-Day invasion, canteen services had to be set up. These were mainly under canvas. The camps were sealed, no-one could enter or leave without special permission, and correspondence was censored. Conditions were primitive, cold and muddy. The only refuge when off duty was often an inadequate portable

HM Queen Elizabeth meets ATS/EFI personnel at Woking depot.

(Photo — NAFFI)

Controller L. V. L. E. Whateley chats with a member of the ATS/EFI, overseas NAAFI girls contingent at their London depot.

(Photo — NAFFI)

First contingent of ATS/EFI ready for overseas posting.

(Photo — NAFFI)

rest hut with a small stove. In spite of the difficulties, the girls kept up morale, both their own and that of the service personnel, and they clamoured to be allowed to cross to France with the invasion forces.

They were soon on French soil — an advance party of 24 landed on 4th August and claim to have caused an unprecedented breach of Army discipline. It was too rough for the troopship to go alongside the Mulberry harbour and consequently they had to disembark at sea. The girls were all wearing battle-dress blouses and skirts. From the bridge came the order, 'Attention all men in the-landing craft — look towards the French shores'. While they did so, the girls climbed over the rail and made their precarious way down the rope ladders. Private Meta Murdock, an ATS/EFI typist, said that each girl received a rousing cheer as she jumped from the swinging ladder into the LST, rising and falling alarmingly on the rough sea. 'It must be the only time so many soldiers disobeyed a direct order,' she wrote afterwards.

In his history of NAAFI, *Service to The Services*, Harry Miller says that, 'The contribution of the NAAFI girls to the comfort and morale of the Forces has never been sufficiently acknowledged outside NAAFI.' Coming from every section of the community and working untiringly 'they kept their nerve and sense of humour under hardship and bombardment'.

Above — from left to right — Miss Agnes Aldred of Leigh, Lancs, Miss C. Cook, Miss N J Fesse, Miss N M Joy in NAAFI Hat, later to be awarded the MBE, Molly Chambers from Blackpool, Lancs.

At the EFI Warrant Officers' and Sergeants' Club in Algiers — Mrs E. O'Shaughnessy of Liverpool, Miss B. Hartley of Redditch, Miss M. Hughes of Barrow-in-Furness, Mrs Gregory of Porthcawl. Mrs O'Shaughnessy met her husband quite by accident in the Algiers' club after she had been working there for 4½ months.
(Photo — NAFFI)

Margaret Scholey who was the first NAAFI girl to volunteer for ATS/EFI. (*Photo – NAFFI*)

NAAFI Uniform – *Reproduced by courtesy of NAAFI*

Overseas canteen girls (ATS/EFI) try on their tropical kit before leaving for NAAFI Middle East canteens. (*Photo – NAFFI*)

142

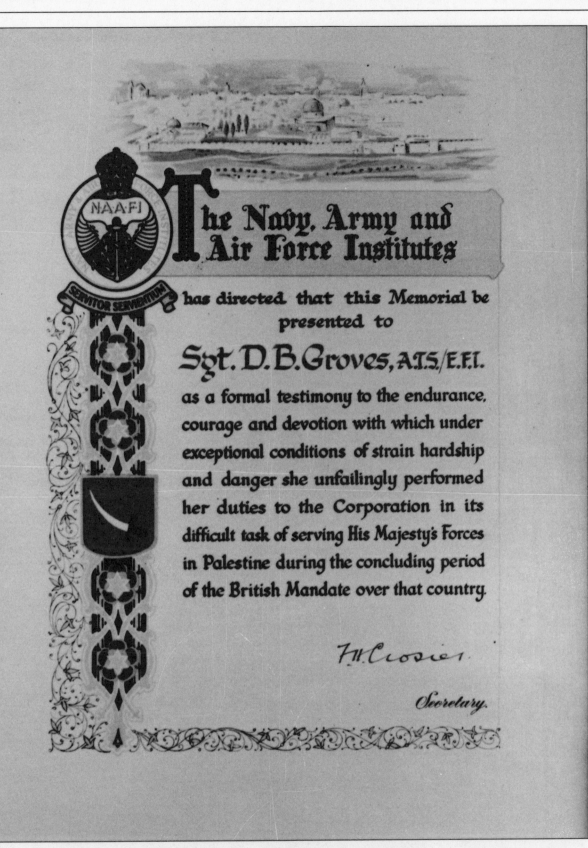

The Navy, Army and Air Force Institutes

has directed that this Memorial be presented to

Sgt. D. B. Groves, A.T.S./E.F.I.

as a formal testimony to the endurance, courage and devotion with which under exceptional conditions of strain hardship and danger she unfailingly performed her duties to the Corporation in its difficult task of serving His Majesty's Forces in Palestine during the concluding period of the British Mandate over that country.

F. H. Crosier.

Secretary.

Sergeant D B Groves Certificate for services in Palastine.

Left – Senior Commander J Cowie.

Below – Enjoying time off in the beautiful botanic gardens in Algiers 1943.
Miss C Legge of Edinburgh, Miss B Smith of Milngavie, Miss B Spence of Nuneaton, Miss C Muir of Glasgow, Miss M Bowen of Swansea, Miss C Cook of Tilicoytry and Miss S Pearse of Killin.

What A Welcome

Right – Driver W Garratt shakes hands with Corporal Lily Brooks, a member of one of the first drafts of the ATS/NAAFI to arrive in Egypt.

Left – What a surprise. A helping hand at the Pyramids.

Left to right – in forage cap Senior Commander M Paton of Perth who has been in Egypt for six years welcomes 2/Sub Kathleen Smith of Bushey and 2/Sub Ruby Brinkley from Brighton, Oct 1943.   (*Photo – NAFFI*)

At the Pyramids of Old Cario, ATS/EFI girls in Egypt 1943.   (*Photo – NAFFI*)

Soldiers', Sailors' and Airmen's Families Association

Above – This was taken on VE day at the Balham Nursery School and shows Evelyn holding the little boy on the pillar.

Below – shows some of the children at Ravenswood SSAFA Childrens Home, Crowthorne, Berkshire.

When the Second World War started, the British Government 'did not anticipate needing their help' but SSAFA thought otherwise and built up its organisation to provide an invaluable link between servicemen and their families at home.

SSAFA was founded in 1885 by Major Gildea of the Warwickshire Regiment. Its initial aim was to look after the families of soldiers going abroad with the Second Egyptian Expeditionary Force. Major Gildea (later to become Colonel Sir James Gildea) was unusual for his time by caring deeply about the welfare of service families. He devoted himself to expanding the association to look after all dependants of Army and Navy personnel. After the formation of the RAF, dependants of Air Force personnel were also included. Because the association was formed first to care for dependants of soldiers, it included "Soldiers" first in its name instead of the Senior Service "Sailors".

The real value of SSAFA in the Second World War began to be seen after Dunkirk and during the bombing. Their Overseas Service provided quick answers to servicemen's queries about their families and their representatives provided emergency help for those in difficulties. Their scope widened steadily, undertaking all aspects of family welfare, opening clothing depots and children's homes and nurseries, wherever the need arose as a result of bombing or evacuation.

By the end of the war SSAFA personnel had grown to nearly 30,000 helpers. Almost all were voluntary. The majority were women and many were the wives of servicemen.

Children Homes for Evacuees

Evelyn Simpson of Canterbury worked in residential homes for evacuees under five years old. Two of which were LCC homes: the Kentish Town Nursery School at Little Durnford Manor near Salisbury and the Balham Nursery School at Sishes End House, Stevenage; one at Bulford Manor, Wiltshire (*which also included children of school age*) and Ravenswood at Crowthorne, Berkshire, were run by SSAFA.

She has happy memories of her days with the children and would like to know what happened to her little friends, especially Terry Bingley who 'loved her ten shillings'.

The Women's Legion

The Women's Legion was founded by Lady Londonderry in the 1914—18 war, but dwindled afterwards. It was revived in 1936 when it concentrated on training which would prepare suitable women as prospective officers when an emergency arose. This revived legion developed into the Women's Emergency Service, headed by Helen Gwynne-Vaughan. The Air Section, which aimed to train instructors, included Pauline Gower and Amy Johnson, who were later to be among the first women pilots in ATA.

When the ATS was launched in 1938, the Women's Emergency Service was able to act in an advisory capacity and was a source of ex- officers with experience in the 1914—18 war, and with training up-dated.

At the outbreak of the Second World War, Lady Londonderry suspended recruitment for the legion and recommended that the younger members should volunteer for one of the women's services. It did not fold up completely, as it offered an outlet for older women who could not make themselves available for mobile work.

The depleted force had more work available than it could well cope with and eventually, when the registration age for women rose to 50, had to request the Ministry of Labour to direct some women in as drivers and canteen workers.

The Owner Driver Section was utilised by the Ministry of Food in Eastern Command, and by the WVS during the evacuation.

The Canteen Service was involved in feeding hundreds of bombed- out people and worked particularly closely with the National Fire Service during the raids on London, until their own catering service was set up.

The Women's Legion was instrumental in the provision of food and drink facilities in air raid shelters — a service which started almost by accident. A canteen crew, taking refreshments to the NFS, was forced to take shelter and found themselves in the midst of 300 enthusiastic customers. Once the need had been observed, it was followed up.

D-Day saw the start of another service — all personnel from Royal Navy and Merchant Navy ships sunk in the Channel were served with hot meals in the Women's Legion canteens when they returned to their depots.

The Mechanical Transport Corps kept its separate identity and operated as the Mechanical Transport Training Corps, under the direction of Mrs G. M. Cook.

Mechanised Transport Corps

When Lady Londonderry advised members of the Women's Legion to volunteer for other women's services, Mrs G. M. Cook and her group of officers in the Mechanical Transport Training Corps did not wish to lose their unit's identity and opted to continue as a voluntary body. At the outbreak of war, Mrs Cook offered the services of the MTTC to the War Office, but this offer was refused.

At first a disappointment, this refusal turned out to be a blessing in disguise, as unrestricted by Government red tape, the MTTC was able to offer its services and undertake work which would have been at worst impossible, and at best slow and difficult to organise had they been under Government control.

In the winter of 1939—40, the French Government accepted their offer of service, and four units went to France; one unit to undertake refugee and evacuation work, plus three ambulance units. One of these units, Hadfield-Spears, remained with the Free French Forces, accompanying them to Tobruk and Italy, and in 1944 landed in France with the Commandos.

Another unit was attached to the Polish Army in UK. One contingent went to Kenya and from there on to Cairo where the units were gradually disbanded or absorbed into the ATS.

By 1943 the Corps, which had changed its title to Mechanised Transport Corps, had expanded to 3,000 members. It was recognised by the Ministry of War Transport, the drivers being paid by the Ministry, and additional women being drafted in.

The Girls Training Corps

The Girls' Training Corps was set up by the Mechanised Transport Corps in 1941 for 16– to 18–year-olds. There was a place for an organisation which would give girls some preliminary basic training, in preparation for their entry into the women's services or to cope with whatever circumstances might confront them in civilian life.

They trained in cooking, first aid, home nursing and fire fighting. In some areas they worked with the WVS, acting as messengers, telephonists, clerical workers, canteen helpers and nursery assistants.

The corps was taken over in 1943 by the National Association of Girls Corps, under the Board of Education.

'Requested . . .'

Barbara Grant was teaching at Hitchin in 1942 and was 'requested' by the headmistress to become an officer of the local Girls' Training Corps, which was just being formed. After a week's training course in London for the officers, the corps was launched. The meetings were held in the school but the girls came from the town. It was necessary to smarten up the girls and teach them to obey orders, so drill was important. Barbara remembers that because she was the youngest and reasonably athletic it was presumed that she would be able to cope. The girls didn't find it easy to accept the discipline of 'hair off the collar' plus marching instead of strolling arm in arm, but they responded well in the end and some became creditable NCOs. Barbara remembers mugging up the Morse code, playing hilarious message-carrying games and marching round Hitchin on parades with other organisations. By the end of the war, as other officers moved on, Barbara rose to the rank of Commandant. She says, 'We all got down to it, wanting to do our bit for victory.'

The photograph shows a GTC parade in Hitchin.

149

The Aims of The Girls Training Corps

The aim of the Girls' Training Corps was: "to provide a general training for national service, primarily for girls of 16–18 years of age, and to equip them in character, body and mind to fulfil their obligation during the War and in the work of reconstruction which must follow". By 1944 there were nearly 1,400 units, with a total of over 55,000 members.

Above – The Wisewood Unit of the GTC learning cookery with Unit Cammander Reynolds.

Below – The Beighton Unit of the GTC undergoing fire fighting practice.

Sergeant Ruby Radley and Sergeant Shelagh Getty enjoying cookery at the Wisewood Unit, The GTC, February 1943.

Parade of the GTC for the visit of His Royal Highness the Duke of Kent to Sheffield.

The various activities of the GTC

Top left – Unit Commander Reynolds (centre) paying a visit during cookery at the Wisewood Unit.

Top right – Learning semaphore with Army instructors at the Beighton Unit.

Middle left – Physical training at the Beighton Unit.

Middle right – Inspection of the Beighton Unit GTC, by the Unit Commander Moore and Unit Commander G. Getty.

Bottom – Members of the Sheffield GTC inspecting model aeroplanes made by ATC recruits.

First Aid Nursing Yeomanry

Apart from nursing units, the First Aid Nursing Yeomanry is the only women's service with continuous existence — it was started in 1909 and did very creditable ambulance duties during the 1914—18 war.

In 1927, FANY was officially recognised by the Army Council as a voluntary reserve transport unit. By the late 1930s the concept was changing and the accent was predominantly on transport rather than on first aid and ambulance work, and the name was amended to Women's Transport Service (FANY).

When the formation of the ATS was under consideration in 1938, it was decided by the Advisory Council that the FANY units should be absorbed into the ATS. The Commandant, Baxter Ellis, and Lady Hailsham, as representative of the FANY Advisory Council were against complete amalgamation but were given no chance to consult further with their council. A verbal agreement was later reached between their Honorary Colonel, General Gibb, and Major General Sir John Brown that FANY Motor Driver Companies should remain as separate entities within ATS, but this unfortunately was not honoured and, after considerable friction, the FANY personnel in the motorised units were absorbed into the ATS. However, the Camberley Training Centre (where Princess Elizabeth was later to train) became, to a large extent, the central focus for FANYs in the ATS, and those volunteers who had enrolled before September 1941 were permitted to wear a sleeve flash "Women's Transport Service FANY". In spite of this very firm time limit, did the number of FANYs seem to increase rather than decrease over the war years, as might have been expected? Perhaps it's tactful not to enquire too closely.

Meanwhile, those FANYs who had not accepted the amalgamation with the ATS — the "Free FANYs" — found many other roles, some temporary and some long-lasting.

There was a Polish unit, to provide canteen facilities, ambulance units, etc. for the Poles coming in large numbers to UK and forming a Polish brigade. Many of the FANYs in this unit were Polish speaking.

With the British Red Cross Society and Order of St John, the FANYs formed driving units for ambulances, etc.

In Finland, the Mediterranean, India, Ceylon and East Africa, FANY units operated. In addition to transport duties, they took responsibility for guarding enemy alien women until they could be repatriated.

Much of the work undertaken by FANY units seemed to start in very casual, informal ways and

Memorial Tablet on
the wall of
St. Paul's Church,
Knightsbridge

1939   1945

IN HONOURED MEMORY OF THOSE MEMBERS OF THE
WOMEN'S TRANSPORT SERVICE (FANY)
WHO GAVE THEIR LIVES FOR THEIR KING AND COUNTRY

M.W. ANDERSON	M. DAMERMENT	M.L.M.McKENZIE MILLIGAN	E.G. SADLER
Y.E.M. BEEKMAN	G.B.M. DICKIE	D. MORGAN	H.I.P. SALMON
D. BEOCH	B.E. EBDEN	R.E. NELSON	J. SHEPLEY
E.M. BOILEAU	M. HEATH-JONES	M.C. PEAKE	L.M. STALKER
A. BORREL	J. HILDICK-SMITH	E.S. PLEWMAN	E.P. STANGER
M.S. BUTLER	N. INYAT-KHAN	B.E. RAMSAY	N.C. STAPYLTON
M. BYCK	C. LEFORT	F.L. RAWLINS	B. SWINBURNE-HANHAM
C.E. CLERK-RATTRAY	V.E. LEIGH	L.V. ROLFE	V.R.E. SZABO
C.D. CROOKE	C.M. LOPRESTI	D.H. ROWDEN	G.M.J. THOMPSON
K. CROSS	D.M. MANNING	Y. RUDELLAT	P.C. WOOLLAN
	NÉE PORTMAN		

W.T.S. (EAST AFRICA)   C.M. BRADFORD (IN JAPAN)

B.M. AUSTIN	B. DUNBAR THOMSON	B. KENTISH	M. SYKES
A. CALLISHER	W. GREY	F.F. MOOJEN	P.H. LE POER TRENCH
H.C. CAMERER	S. HOOK	R. SOUTHEY	

THEIR NAME LIVETH FOR EVERMORE.

their involvement with Special Operations Executive came about in such a way. Soon after the fall of France, Major General Sir Colin Gubbins (then Colonel Gubbins) rang FANY HQ and asked if two FANYs could be provided for 'rather special confidential work' which might continue for some time. Phyllis Bingham, secretary to Marian Gamwell, who had recently assumed command, had taken the call and, as she was known to Colonel Gubbins, Marian Gamwell suggested that she should go and choose another FANY to accompany her. Their first work was packing in small containers, detonators, explosive and all materials required to blow bridges, etc. which were intended for use by the Home Guard in the event of invasion.

From this almost chance beginning grew a very wide involvement in all aspects of the SOE – the training centres were entirely staffed on the domestic side by FANYs, they provided much of the necessary office staff and they manned the transport. The whole of SOE was completely blanketed in secrecy and it was not until after the war that the involvement of FANY was known – their silence on their work had been complete throughout.

Names like Violette Szabo, Odette Churchill, Christine Granville and Nancy Wake are famous but without the back-up provided to such a high degree of efficiency by their fellow members, their work would have been infinitely more taxing.

Towards the end of the war, the Free FANYs were invited by the War Office to assist in providing welfare workers in South East Asia Command. This was the first direct approach by the War Office

Nancy Wake, an Austrialian, was married to a Frenchman. She worked with the Resistance, but eventually had to escape to England. She joined SOE, parachuted into the Auvergne, where she organised and fought with the Marquis until the end of the War, winning many decorations from Britain and France.

to the FANYs and the response was immediate, and valuable work was done – some of it unexpectedly dramatic.

Joan Bamford-Fletcher, a Canadian who had come to England to join the FANYs and had spent some years with the Polish Army in Scotland, was in the first contingent to go to SEAC, and in October 1945 she was landed in Sumatra to evacuate internees from Bangkinang Camp.

It was a mammoth task – she made a 90 kilometre trip over 5,000 feet mountains 20 times in 30 days, using a "task force" of Japanese military personnel who were more than a little startled to find themselves under the command of a woman. The roads were bad, the vehicles broke down repeatedly, the Indonesians were hostile and the situation was so bad that the last convoy had to be guarded by 70 Japanese soldiers armed with machine guns. After one hair-raising encounter with some 500 hostile Indonesians, Joan said: 'I must say I was rather glad to get out of that hole!'

She earned the admiration of the Japanese soldiers (but they said they would never marry European women – they were too tough) and was presented with his 300-year-old sword by the Captain of a transport unit.

The FANY also provided canteen facilities for British and Indian units in Japan, under extremely difficult conditions.

In spite of initial difficulties with Government departments and lack of full official recognition, whatever FANYs were called on to undertake was carried out with efficiency and complete dedication.

Elaine Plewman, She was parachuted into France in 1943 to help establish a new circuit in Marseilles. She was arrested in March 1944. She was cruelly used, but did not give away any names, and was executed in Dachau concentration Camp in September 1944.

Special Operations Executive

The Special Operations Executive was conceived on 19th July 1940 when Churchill drafted a memorandum for his War Cabinet, concerning the creation of a body 'to co-ordinate all action by way of subversion and sabotage against the enemy overseas'. He later put it more succinctly as, 'to set Europe ablaze'.

Before SOE could be put into action, he sent a message to Anthony Eden, the War Secretary, which considerably widened the terms of reference: 'It is, of course, urgent and indispensable that every effort should be made to obtain secretly the best possible information about the German forces in the various countries overrun, and to establish intimate contacts with local people and to plant agents. This, I hope is being done on the largest scale as opportunity serves by the new organisation under the Ministry of Economic Warfare.'

So the work of the SOE began, and built up to a scale which could not have been anticipated at its inception, in a field undreamed of before the war. All the members of "the Org" were volunteers and came from a wide range of backgrounds; many of them had no connection with the armed forces and the military "Top Brass" was aghast at this use of "amateurs" who knew nothing of war (as they knew it). They were even more horrified at the quite outrageous step of accepting and training women for the work.

The stories of some of these women are sufficiently well known through books, films and television not to need retelling here – Violette Szabo and Odette have become symbols of the courage and endurance of women.

The Special Training Centres for SOE personnel were staffed by members of FANY, first on the domestic side. Since the strictest secrecy had to be observed, all the work had to be in the hands of an organisation whose absolute discretion could be guaranteed. In time they became more and more involved in the administrative work and some eventually trained as agents.

Some of the agents recruited were enrolled in the FANY or the WAAF, and another group were drawn from WAAF personnel. One WAAF squadron officer came to be a pivot of the French section. Vera Atkins collected every scrap of current information she could about life in France – work, travel, curfews, food rationing, police registrations, etc. – and amassed a collection of the small, everyday items which could add credence to the cover stories of the agents. She also played a prominent part in maintaining contact with agents in the field. For five years she gave all her time, thought and energy to the French section and was described as 'cool, extremely competent and analytical' and as 'the real brain of the French section'. Because of her care for the morale and welfare of the agents and their families, she could also be said to have been the heart of the section. After the war she toured the German concentration camps, investigating the records of missing agents, and through her work the fate of most of the women was established. She has continued to help those who were in the field.

The fate of many of the agents was horrific in the extreme – few who were captured by the Gestapo survived, and it is known that most were tortured before they were killed. Little or no information was divulged by the agents under torture.

Odette – Mrs Peter Churchill, GC, MBE – was captured on her first mission to France in 1943. She was imprisoned in various prisons and concentration camps, where she was barbarously tortured, but lived to the end of the war and release.

Lilian Rolfe, courier to a résau in Orleans, was in Ravensbruck with Violette Szabo and Denise Black, a French Jewess who had escaped from France and returned as a radio operator in 1944. They were shot and cremated together.

Peggy Knight had only a short spell in France but an eventful one. She entered the country by parachute in April 1944. After D-Day she was cycling round from camp to camp, arranging the reception of arms and carrying messages into Paris. She took part in an ambush on a German lorry convoy. Acting as a courier between FFI units and British and American forces, she crossed the German lines several times and was interrogated by the Germans.

Vera Leigh, daughter of an American father and English mother, lived in France. She began helping stranded British soldiers and shot-down RAF crews to escape. By 1942 the Gestapo was searching for her and she used the escape route

Diana Rowden had lived for many years in France. When the war started she joined the WAAF but was transferred to SOE. She was landed by Lysander in June 1943 and operated as courier to a circuit in The Jura. She was captured at the end of November, held in Karlsruhe prison and in July 1944 was burned alive in the crematorium at Natzweiler. She was post-humously awarded the Croix de Guerre.

herself, but was arrested at the Spanish border. She spent some weeks in an internment camp but eventually reached England via Gibraltar. She trained with SOE and by mid-summer 1943 was back in Paris, but only five months later was lured to a rendezvous, arrested and taken to Fresnes prison where, with Diana Rowden and Sonia Olschanesky, she was injected with phenol and cremated.

Only a very small number of the stories of courage is it possible to tell, but they are sufficient for us to realise with amazement that women looked at the possible dangers and still undertook the missions asked of them. Patriotic and courageous are inadequate descriptions. They are bright stars in the history of British women.

Violette Szabo was sent twice to occupied France. On her second assignment she was captured, tortured and did not return from Ravensbruck when the war ended. She never gave any information which could endanger her comrades.

Other Lands, Other Service

British women in other countries also took the opportunities which opened to help our war effort.

Do you have a fuchsia in a hanging basket, with rose-red tube and sepals and white corolla, named Audrey Hepburn? If so, did you know that it was not named as a tribute to her as an actress or to mark her work with UNICEF, but in remembrance of her work as a dedicated teenager who worked for the Dutch patriots?

Audrey Hepburn's English father and Dutch mother had parted before the Second World War and she had been living in England, but in 1939 her mother thought she would be safer in Holland. Her mother was deeply involved with the Dutch underground, and at 13 Audrey Hepburn was dancing at small and very private concerts to raise money for this work. She was studying at the Arnhem Conservatoire of Music which became an important front for concealing Dutch patriots. The students, too young to be suspected by the Germans, carried messages for the underground. As she spoke both Dutch and English, Audrey Hepburn was of special importance and, after the landing at Arnhem, she acted as interpreter and mes-

senger for the British and is remembered as outstanding in bringing aid and comfort to beleaguered soldiers. Arnhem was still a battlefield — daunting work for a 16–year-old to undertake.

In Chamonix, two elderly ladies were the only English people left. Miss Forrest and Miss Wood had trained as missionaries at the Faith Mission in Edinburgh, and when war came they remained in Chamonix in their very English little home, quietly continuing their work in the small mission hall. So unobtrusive were they that the fact that they were hiding escaped prisoners of war and helping them to freedom over the mountains never roused any suspicions. They enlisted the help of mountain guides — these guides, they said, were famous and, 'We know the guides — we know everyone in Chamonix. They are our friends. We often have them to tea.' They began their escape route independently but later were incorporated into the "regular" service. After the war, those who knew of their work tried to ensure that they were honoured for it, but Miss Forrest and Miss Wood would not hear of it — 'Anyone would have done the same under the circumstances,' they said.

Gladys Aylward was a missionary in China for 20 years, and when the Japanese invaded she led 100 children from the mission school over mountainous country to safety. Shown here some of the children before they crossed the mountains to Siam.

Gladys Aylward

In the spring of 1939 Freya Stark, then living in Italy, wrote to the Foreign Office to ask if her Arabic could be of any use and, as a result, spent six years in the Middle East and Italy, going out first to Aden as Assistant Intelligence Officer in October. Italy had not yet entered the war, but fascist propaganda was at its peak and there was a considerable German presence. In her diary she says, 'The fascists are bringing all their guns to bear on me.' From Aden she went to Cairo and, after a short spell there, went on to Iraq. She was in Baghdad during the Iraq revolution and described the siege of the British Embassy vividly in her book *Dust In The Lions Paw*.

During May and June 1941, the Embassy was isolated. Iraqi officers were sent on 3rd May to remove their wireless (but Freya Stark records, 'they did not find all'). The electric supply and telephones were cut off. There was bombing, shelling and sniping around the Embassy but in spite of all the privations, no casualties. At the end of the siege the entry in her diary reads: 'The riot has died down . . . sat this afternoon quietly embroidering on the lawn . . . pleasant peace!'

At the other side of the world, a small woman (who as a girl had worked as a parlourmaid in London, dreaming of being a missionary in China) led 100 children out of the hands of the Japanese to safety over the mountains. Gladys Aylward did

Canadian girls working in British Embassy, Military Missions, etc. in Washington. Many Canadian girls tried to enlist in some organisation which would bring them to Europe but when this proved impossible looked for war work in Washington.

intelligence work for the Nationalists, as well as caring for the children in the mission. After the town was bombed they lived in caves for some weeks but when she heard that the Japanese had put a price on her head, she started on her incredible journey. She had no money and very little food but she had an unshakeable determination not to let her beloved children fall into the hands of the advancing Japanese army. With no other adult to help her, she shepherded 100 children across country which was a virtual battlefield and over trackless mountain ranges, depending on what food they could beg or find *en route*.

In all theatres of war and in every occupied country, British women, caught in the devastation of war did whatever it lay within their power to do, often putting what they saw as their duty before their own safety. Some, like Frau Z., an English-woman married to a German, were proud of their British nationality – her daughter told me that she was often terrified because her mother would re-prove anyone she heard denigrating the British. Some, like Margaret, schooling herself not to speak a word of English in case a chance word from her or her small children might draw un-welcome attention and perhaps risk her Dutch husband's work with the underground being uncovered.

In their own way, in their own circumstances, they just got on with it too.

A DAILY OCCURENCE . . .

Women from all parts of the Commonwealth wanted to play their part – many of the overseas Army and Air Force units brought their own womens' corps. Canadian girls filled many vacancies in expanding British Embassy and Military and Trade Mission Offices.

Rain or shine, is the line-up in front of a Washington cafeteria at lunchtime. Here are Doris Beverley, Doreen Anderson, Molly Adamson, Isabel O'Donnell, Margaret Bartuah, all of Toronto.

Conclusion

All this and much more, the women of these islands did between 1939 and 1945. I have tried to show how wide the scope of their contribution was, but I am sure someone somewhere will say, 'but she hasn't mentioned what I was doing'.

In 1941, in *British Women At War*, Mary Cox wrote, 'Even if it were possible to give a full account of the activities of all the women's organisations, and the way in which these have been extended to assist the country's war needs, a wealth of work would still remain unrecorded for the resource, endurance and practical competence of the women of Britain working on their own in building up as formidable an addition to the war strength of the country as is derived from any other source,' and she goes on to say that the women 'who carry on triumphantly showing the world that British women can not only "take it", but take it with a smile, are a fighting force which may well prove decisive in the war of nerves, which is hardly less vital than the war of steel and oil'.

There was little feeling that we were doing anything splendid. The work was there and somebody had to do it, that was clear, and who else was there to do it? We might be asked to do work which bored us, we might be asked to go on working when we were more tired than we knew it was possible to be, but there was a supportive feeling that we were all pulling together, and the alternative to eventual victory was so unthinkable that we saw no alternative to sticking it and STICKING IT until the war ended.

One can only repeat the words of Lady Reading in her message to the WVS at the end of the war: 'We have learned that it is no good talking about things, we must do them. We have done work we had never thought to do. We know now that in life no obstacle can block, it can only impede; that tiredness is an incident, not a finality.'

In short, we just got on with it!

Appendix

Reproduced here are the main topics from: VAD Form 11. Issued 19 January 1940

648048   V.A.D. Form 11.

No.

19 JAN 19

WILTSHIRE

DRESS REGULATIONS

AND EQUIPMENT LIST

for

Officers and Members

of

Voluntary Aid Detachments

on Mobilization

I. COUNTY OFFICIALS.

(1).—County Controllers. On mobilization a pattern of service uniform will be authorised for the use of those County Controllers who are not entitled to wear any service uniform as an Officer.

(2).—Assistant County Controllers. On mobilization a pattern of service uniform will be authorised for the use of those Assistant County Controllers who are not entitled to wear the uniform of one of the Bodies.

II. MEN.

(3).—Men—Mobile Men Members. Mobile men members will be issued with a complete set of service uniform on enlistment. They are therefore not required to join in uniform.

(4).—Men—Immobile Men Members will continue to wear the prescribed uniform, badges and shoulder titles of their own unit of the St. John Ambulance Brigade, St. Andrew's Ambulance Association or the British Red Cross Society, as the case may be for the whole period of mobilization. (For scale see Appendix A.)

III. WOMEN.

(5).—Women—Mobile and Immobile Members. All women members will join in and continue to wear the prescribed uniform, badges and shoulder titles of their own unit of the St. John Ambulance Brigade, St. Andrew's Ambulance Association or British Red Cross Society as the case may be, for the whole period of mobilization. (For scale see Appendix B.)

(6).—Women Officers and Section Leaders volunteering for duty as nursing members must wear the uniform of a member unless other instructions are given.

(7).—*Uncertificated Nursing Members (Grade I) may be required to replace members of the Nursing Services and will then be entitled to wear as a distinguishing badge the letters " G.I." in the form of a brooch on the shoulder straps of the great coat and on the bib of the apron on indoor uniform.

(8).—Geneva Brassard, Identity Certificate and Respirator. All Mobile Members, before proceeding abroad, will be issued with a Geneva Brassard, identity certificate and respirator under arrangements to be made by the Service concerned.

IV. GRANTS FOR UNIFORM AND EQUIPMENT (WOMEN).

(9).—Initial Upkeep Grants for Uniform have been authorised for those posted to duty as Officers or other ranks.

(10).—Commandants, Assistant Commandants and Quartermasters, serving as such will receive an initial grant of £20 for uniform.

---

*For definition see " General & Training Regulations for Voluntary Aid Detachments," para. 52(1).

3

(11).—Certificated Nurses and Nursing Members receive an initial grant of £10 and upkeep grant of £5 for uniform.

(12).—Non-Nursing Members receive an initial grant of £8, and upkeep grant of £4 for uniform.

(13).—Immobile Members will be eligible for the grants shown above and if employed as Nursing Members will be eligible to receive washing allowance.

(14).—Grants will be paid direct to the Officer or Member if and when the appointment is confirmed, and amounts will be subject to variation in the light of prices and conditions prevailing at the time of mobilization. The upkeep grant will be issued in two portions, 75% and 25% alternatively, every six months : the first issue being made at the beginning of the thirteenth month of service.

(15).—†Active Service Allowance. Mobile Nursing Members are eligible for an active service outfit allowance of £8 5s. od., payable before they proceed on active service. Members ordered abroad will claim their active service outfit allowance from the appropriate Command Paymaster through the Officer commanding the unit with which they are serving.

(16).—Camp Kit Allowance. All members proceeding abroad to stations where Camp kit is required will receive a Camp kit allowance of £7 10s. od.

V. GENERAL.

(17).—Uniform must be worn at all times ; the wearing of plain clothes is forbidden. Hospital authorities and V.A.D. Officers have the right to insist on uniforms being correctly worn and will receive the support of the V.A.D. Council in so doing.

(18).—Identity Discs will be supplied to all members called up for service on mobilization whether at home or abroad. The Officer Commanding the Hospital which they join for service will make the issue, this paragraph of the Regulations being quoted as the authority to supply.

(19).—Uniform Certificate Forms. Officers and members may be called upon to produce their uniform certificate form on any occasion when required by a competent authority so to do.

---

†Washing Allowance. Certificated Nurses and Nursing Members employed on mobilization are eligible to receive washing allowance at 3/6d. per week.
Non-Nursing Members will receive washing allowance at 2/6d. per week.

4

(20).—Marking. Every garment must be clearly marked with full name.

(21).—Personal Uniform and Equipment includes the equipment which may be authorised for the personal use of members and which they would take with them when attached to or transferred from one Service unit to another.

(22).—Clothing and Necessaries comprise the personal kit of the Officer or member other than equipment.

(23).—Part Time Duty. Members who are only required for part time duty will not be eligible to receive upkeep or initial grants for uniform.

(24).—Return of Uniform. The uniform of any Officer or member ceasing to be employed through his or her own fault will be returned to the Secretary of the V.A.D. Council.

VI. APPENDIX A.

List of Articles of Personal Uniform and Equipment to be brought by Immobile Men Members when called up on mobilization.

The uniform in question will be that of the Body to which the member belongs, the Regulations of which are to be strictly observed.

   1 Great Coat.
   1 Jacket.
   1 pair Knickerbocker breeches and puttees, or trousers.
   1 Cap.
   1 pair Boots.
   1 pair Gloves.
   Sam Browne Belt, white linen collars and black tie (Officers only).
   1 Haversack.
   1 Waterbottle.

It must be understood that no official upkeep grants have been authorised for the above.

VII. APPENDIX B.

List of Articles of Personal Uniform and Equipment to be brought by Mobile Women Members when called up on mobilization.

The uniform in question will be that of the Body to which the members belong, the Regulations of which are to be strictly observed.

5

NURSING MEMBERS.

Indoor Uniform.

3 Dresses.
12 Aprons.
3 Belts.
6 Collars.
3 pairs Cuffs *or* 3 pairs Sleeves.
4 Caps.
2 pairs Ward Shoes (Sensible soles, moderate heels), black.
6 pairs Stockings, non-transparent, black.
1 pair scissors.

Outdoor Uniform.

1 Greatcoat.
1 pair Gloves, grey or white.
1 Hat *or* Gabardine Cap.
1 Cardigan, grey or dark blue.
1 Waterproof.
1 Jacket and skirt.
2 Shirt blouses, white, navy blue or grey.
1 Tie.   } Advised.
1 Belt.
1 Off duty Dress.
Walking shoes (sensible soles, moderate heels), black.
1 Suit case. Underclothing and personal necessaries—including soap.
2 Towels (hand).
2 Towels (bath).

IX. APPENDIX D.

List of Articles for which the Active Service Outfit Allowance is issued. (Nursing Members only).

1 Suit case, 30 inches by 24 inches by 12 inches.
1 Hold-all.
1 Rug.
1 Cushion.
1 Looking-glass.
1 Small Oil Stove and Kettle.
1 Small Candle Lantern.
1 pair Gum Boots.
1 Flat Iron.
1 Roll-up, containing knife, fork, dessert spoon and teaspoon.
1 Cup and Saucer.
1 Tea Infuser.
Secure Tent Pole Strap.

Instruments.
2 pairs Scissors.
2 pairs Forceps.
2 Clinical Thermometers.

VIII. APPENDIX C.

NON-NURSING MEMBERS.

1 Greatcoat.
1 Jacket and skirt.
1 Hat or Gabardine Cap.
8 Collars, white.
3 Shirt blouses, white, navy blue or grey.
1 Belt.
1 Tie.
1 Cardigan, grey or dark blue.
3 Coats, white (for all except Hospital Cooks, Cooks and Clerks).
6 Overalls, white (for Hospital Cooks, Cooks and Clerks).
5 Caps (Hospital Cooks, and Cooks only).
6 pairs Stockings, non-transparent, black.
2 pairs Shoes (sensible soles, moderate heels), black.
1 Suit case, underclothing and personal necessaries—including soap.

6

X. APPENDIX E.

List of Articles for which the Camp Kit Allowance is issued.

1 Portable Camp Bedstead.
1 Bag for above.
1 Pillow.
1 Waterproof Sheet, 7ft. by 4ft. 6 inches.
1 Tripod Washstand with Proofed Basin, Bath and Bag.
1 Folding Chair.
1 Waterproof Bucket.
1 Valise or Kit Bag to hold the above-mentioned articles with the owner's name painted upon it.

Members are requested to note that no furniture is provided for their individual use ; it is therefore imperative that they provide themselves with the above Camp Kit. The above articles must be purchased from The Army & Navy Stores, Ltd., 105, Victoria Street, Westminster, London, S.W.1.

All orders will be promptly dealt with by these Headquarters on receipt of a telegram or telephone message or letter addressed to Camp Equipment and marked " V.A.D."

7

Bibliography

Babington-Smith, Constance, *Evidence in Camera* David and Charles, 1957.

Beauman, Katherine Bentley, *Partners in Blue*.

Beauman, Katherine Bentley, *Wings on Her Shoulders* Hutchinson, 1943.

Bidwell, Shelford, *W.R.A.C. (Famous Regiments)* Leo Cooper, 1977.

Bielenberg, Christabel, *The Past is Myself* Chatto and Windus, 1968.

Billingham, Elizabeth, *Civial Defence in War* Murray, London, 1941.

Booth, D.P., *Women at War: Engineering* John Crowther Publications, 1943.

Bowden Jean, *Grey Touched with Scarlet* Robert Hale, 1957.

Burton, Elaine, *What of the Women?* Frederick Muller Ltd., 1941.

Cole, Lt.Col. Howard N., *N.A.A.F.I. in Uniform* The Forces Press (N.A.A.F.I.), 1982.

Cookridge, E.H., *Inside S.O.E.* Arthur Barker Ltd., 1946.

Cooper, Page, *Navy Nurse* Whittlesey House, 1946.

Cox, Mary, *British Women at War* John Murray & The Pilot Press, 1941.

Curtis, Lettice, *Forgotten Pilots* Nelson and Saunders Ltd., 1971.

Dean, Basil, *Theatre at War* George G. Harrup, 1948

Douie, Vera, *Daughters of Britain* Ronald, 1950.

Drummond, John D., *Blue for a Girl, the Story of the W.R.N.S.* W.H.Allen, 1960.

Escott, Sqn.Ldr. Beryl E., *Women in Air Force Blue* Patrick Stephens Ltd., 1989.

Fitzgibbon, Constantine, *The Blitz* Wingate, 1951.

Graves, Charles, *Women in Green.* Heinemann, 1948

Fletcher, M.H., *The W.R.N.S.* B.T.Batsford Ltd., 1989.

Foot, M.R.D., *S.O.E. in France.* HMSO, 1966

Gwynne Vaughan, Dame Helen, *Service With the Army.*

Hall, Pat, *What a Way to Win a War* Midas Books, Tunbridge Wells, 1978.

Harland, Kathleen, 'Queen Alexandra's Royal Naval Nursing Service' *Journal of the Royal Naval Medical Service* u.d.

Harrison, Ada M. (ed), *Grey and Scarlet* Hodder and Stoughton, 1948.

Haslett, Caroline, *Munitions Girl; Handbook for Women of the Industrial Army* English U.P., 1942.

Hay, Ian, *One Hundred Years of Army Nursing* Cassell, 1953.

Hodgson, Vera, *Few Eggs and no Oranges* Dobson, 1946.

Hodson, James Lansdale, *Home Front* Gollancz, 1944.

Hughes, John Graven, *The Greasepaint War* New English Library, 1976.

Izzard, Molly, *A Heroine in Her time* Macmillan, 1969.

Jackson, Carlton, *Who Will Take Our Children* Methuen, 1985.

Longmate, Norman, *How We Lived Then* Hutchinson of London, 1971.

MacDonald, *Red Tape Notwithstanding* Hutchinson, 1941.

McBride, Brenda, *Quiet Heroines* Chatto and Windus, 1985.

Mason, Ursula Stuart, *The W.R.N.S., 1917–1977* Educational Explorers, 1977.

'Meet the Members' Bennett, Bristol, 1945.

Miller, Harry, *Service to the Services* Newman Neame, London, 1971.

Matthews, Vera Laughton, *Blue Tapestry* Hollis & Carter, 1948.

Priestley, J.B., *British Women Go To War* Collins, 1943.

Sackville-West, V.M., *The W.L.A.* Joseph, 1944.

Scott, Peggy, *They Made Invasion Possible* Hutchinson, 1944.

Stafford, Ann, *Army Without Banners* Collins, 1942.

Stark, Freya, *Dust in the Lions Paw* Century, 1985.

Tancred, E., *Women Police. 1914–1950* National Council of Women of Great Britain, 1951.

Taylor, Eric, *Women Who Went to War* Robert Hale, London, 1988.

Terry, Ray, *Women in Khaki* Columbus Books, 1988.

Titmus, Richard, *Official Histoy of the Second World War* H.M.S.O. & Longman, 1950.

Townsend, Colin and Eileen, *War Wives* Grafton Books, 1989.

Wadge, *Women in Uniform* Sampson Low, 1946.

Ward, Dame Irene, *F.A.N.Y.* Invicta/Hutchinson, 1955.

Williams-Ellis, Annabel, *Women in War Factories* Gollancz, 1943.

Winslow, T.E., *Forwarned is Forearmed. A History of the Royal Observer Corps* William Hodge & Co., 1948.

Wood, Derek, *Attack Warning Red* Janes, 1976.

Woolfitt, Susan, *Idle Women* Benn, 1947.